FIELDS
AND
HEDGEROWS

FIELDS
AND
HEDGEROWS
A NATURE
· GUIDE ·

BRIAN LEE

The Crowood Press

A school teacher by profession, Brian Lee
writes a regular column on farming and
wildlife topics for the British Naturalists'
Association's magazine *Country-Side*.

First published in 1985 by
The Crowood Press
Ramsbury, Marlborough,
Wiltshire SN8 2HE

Reprinted in paperback 1989

British Library Cataloguing in Publication Data

Lee, Brian, 1947–
    (Guide to fields, farms and hedgerows).
    Fields and hedgerows
    1. Great Britain. Urban regions. Organisms
    I. Title II. British Naturalists' Association
    574.941

    ISBN 1–85223–234–X

Design by Vic Giolitto

Typeset by Quadraset Limited, Midsomer Norton,
Bath, Avon
Printed in Spain by Graficromo s.a., Cordoba

Contents

FOREWORD

Since 1905 the British Naturalists' Association has provided opportunities for beginners and more advanced students of natural history to rub shoulders with experts, both amateur and professional.

Throughout this time its magazine, *Country-Side*, and its local, regional and national meetings have fostered the collection and sharing of knowledge concerning the rocks, soils, plants and animals which make up our living landscape. Essential in this process of national learning and the spreading of awareness about wildlife has been the publication of many identification keys – keys to groups like lichens, plant galls, harvestmen and spiders, which though present and often abundant in most habitats were at one time frequently overlooked or wrongly ignored, because there was no way in, no key to unlock the doors of enquiry. In the same way, the Association's pamphlets entitled 'Let's begin the study of . . .' helped pioneer many branches of field science.

At last, some of that knowledge, the fruit of all those eighty years of unique experience, is now made public in this superb series of books. Habitat by habitat, all is revealed.

Most of my own knowledge of plants and animals was gained in the field by walking with and listening to the 'ologists', the experts in each subject – bryology, ornithology, algology etc, etc. Each trip was an occasion to be remembered thanks to the personal anecdotes and sheer enthusiasm of people who had all the facts at their fingertips and who loved the subject of their expertise.

If you can't go on such trips, these books are the next best thing. Open up the pages and you can almost smell the sweet or rotten smell of a river, see the rooks flying from the beech hangers, and hear the warm buzz of summer insects or the crisp crackle of a winter morning.

If I may be allowed one personal reminiscence. I can remember following John Clegg (the author of the volume on ponds and streams in this series) down to the ponds in the grounds of Haslemere Educational Museum, where he was then curator. *Stratiotes aloides* (water soldier), *Nepa cinerea* (the water scorpion), *Hydrocharis morsus ranae* (frogbit), *Gunnera manicata* (the giant prickly rhubarb from South America). . . . This was the first time I was ever shown these things and I will never forget either the experience or the names.

I am grateful to John Clegg and all the others who led me along the many paths of natural history and to a very full and worthwhile life. I am grateful too to all the officers and members of the British Naturalists' Association, both past and present, for everything they have done and are doing to share their knowledge and wonder of life.

What a super series of books! The only problem is what is the B.N.A. going to do to celebrate its centenary?

David Bellamy

*President of the Youth Section of
the British Naturalists' Association*
Bedburn, County Durham

 **British Naturalists' Association**

The British Naturalists' Association has existed since 1905, when E. Kay Robinson founded the B.N.A.'s journal *Country-Side* and groups of readers began to hold meetings which gave amateur naturalists an opportunity to meet experts and to discuss topics of mutual interest with them. It is this network of branches all over Britain that forms the basis of the B.N.A. New members are always welcome and enquiries regarding membership should be addressed to Mrs June Pearton, 48 Russell Way, Higham Ferrers, Northamptonshire NN9 8EJ.

During its eighty years of existence many distinguished naturalists and public figures have been associated with the B.N.A. At present the President is Lord Skelmersdale, the President of the Youth Section is David Bellamy, and R.S.R. Fitter, Eric Hosking, Alfred Leutscher, Professor Kenneth Mellanby, Angela Rippon, Sir Peter Scott, Professor T.R.E. Southwood, Sir George Taylor and H.J. Wain are Vice-Presidents of the Association.

Country-Side appears four times a year and publishes articles about every aspect of natural history. Contributions, including photographs and drawings, should be addressed to Ron Freethy, The Editor, *Country-Side*, Thorneyholme Hall, Roughlee, Nr Burnley, Lancashire BB12 9LH.

INTRODUCTION

Few people realise that the landscape which we think of as 'natural' is, with rare exceptions, not natural at all but is man-made – the product of generations of toil which have imposed man's pattern on the face of the countryside. At first our exploitation of nature, brought about by need for food, clothing and shelter, was so tentative and on such a small scale that the impact we made on our environment was insignificant. But later, as the population increased, change became more rapid and wildlife began to be affected to a greater degree. As successive generations prospered and multiplied, added strains were placed on the farming community as it strived to keep pace with the ever-growing demand for food.

Chapter 1 traces how agriculturists rose to the challenge by constantly improving implements, seeds, stock and farming methods, changing the face of the countryside in the process. The development of enclosure and the use of marginal land all contributed to greater success, as did the more recent introduction of pesticides, weedkillers and artificial fertilisers – although their use has been responsible for side effects harmful to wildlife and the countryside.

Subsequent chapters describe some of the species of wildlife which are found on farmland today and discuss, where appropriate, the relationship between agriculture and wildlife, including some traditional uses of the produce of the countryside.

Opinion about any environmental question always seems to be divided into opposing factions, each unwilling to concede that there is any sense or truth in the opposition's views. The farming versus wildlife controversy is no exception. What the extremists on both sides cannot see is that farming and wildlife can and must coexist – for farming cannot thrive in an ecologically sterile environment.

It has therefore been my aim to outline for naturalists some of the problems faced by farmers and, conversely, to explain to farmers why conservation is vital in order to maintain a balanced ecological system, so that the countryside is viewed neither as a food factory nor as a wildlife museum but as a live and ever-changing resource able to provide both food and enjoyment.

1 THE SHAPING OF THE LAND

After the great ice age, about 8,000 years ago, as the climate became warmer and drier, the tundra receded and dense woodlands of pine, hazel, oak, elm and lime clothed the valleys. Alders and willows colonised damp areas. Deer grazed the grasslands and wild boar rooted for acorns in forest clearings. Some of these clearings may not have been natural, although there is little evidence to prove conclusively that man was beginning to clear forest in order to keep animals or grow crops at such an early date. However, by Neolithic times forest clearance was taking place on a larger scale to provide grazing areas for animals and land for crops. Man had begun to shape the landscape – a process which has continued to the present day. The countryside which is so much admired by the naturalist is, except for its natural undulations, almost entirely a man-made environment.

About 4000 BC, the Neolithic people came to Britain, introducing a higher culture which was primarily based on a new technique of shaping and polishing stone implements by using coarse-grained stones to grind a more exact shape and a sharper edge than had previously been possible. Because they made better tools, Neolithic people were able to develop a wider range of skills, which included new methods of agriculture and the domestication of animals including cattle, sheep, goats and pigs.

Neolithic people were still hunters as well as farmers and it is very likely that they continued to live a semi-nomadic existence. Clearings were probably made by ring-barking trees, a much easier job than felling. When the fertility of a clearing declined, new

areas were cleared. Neolithic farmers grew crops, including wheat, barley and linseed. Storage bins for grain and seed crops have been found by archaeologists, and sickles from the period have also been found.

As the Neolithic people prospered and their population increased there was a greater demand for agricultural land and new methods of forest clearance had to be adopted. Carbon dating techniques on traces of charcoal and other remains have revealed that burning was used to clear large areas of forest from about 3500 BC onwards. Pollen analysis shows a marked decrease in the amount of elm and a great increase in the pollen of plantains or ribworts (Plantaginaceae) and members of the Chenopodiaceae (goosefoot, fat hen), which thrive in cultivated ground. Areas of East Anglia and many of the moors of northern England were cleared by Neolithic farmers and have been open land ever since, although many people think they have always been so. No doubt the soil was soon exhausted and the farming community moved on. There is no evidence that Neolithic people developed long-term farming communities but archaeologists have found proof that Neolithic farmers used a primitive form of plough – perhaps the most significant implement in the shaping of the landscape until the invention of the bulldozer.

When South Street Long Barrow at Avebury in Wiltshire was excavated, the soil beneath the barrow showed signs of grooving in two directions, at right angles. Carbon 14 dating indicated that the plough grooves were made about 3000 BC. Indeed, the ploughed field existed in Britain 5,000 years ago,

Above The plough, the shaper of the landscape.

Opposite (top) Tamworth pigs bear a distinct resemblance to their wild boar ancestors.

Opposite (bottom) An ancient woodland clearing.

though we do not know whether the fields were open or were enclosed by walls or hedges.

The plough was merely a branch with another branch fixed to it at right angles or a sharp stone attached to the end furthest from the operator, who pulled the implement towards himself and scratched the surface of the soil. It was known as a crook-ard. A similar type of plough, perhaps drawn by oxen, remained in use for thousands of years. One slight development was the beam-ard, which had an arrow-shaped ploughshare. The beam-ard, however, could still only scratch the soil and was incapable of turning over the ground or bringing subsoil to the surface.

Another major factor in the development of farming has been the changing pattern of field systems and the ways in which field boundaries were defined by hedges, walls, hurdles and fences. Near settlements small stone compounds were built to stop animals from straying and to protect them from scavenging wolves. Arable land needed to be defined and there is evidence that some prehistoric fields were marked by heaps of stones rather than being surrounded by walls. In areas in the south of England, where suitable rock could be found, boundary walls were constructed in the form of rows of standing stones. Inadvertently, man was providing a suitable nesting habitat for the birds which are now commonly associated with walls and buildings. Some walls were constructed as a way of disposing of stones and rubble excavated during the course of cultivating the land.

A distinguishing feature of prehistoric field systems is the occurrence of lynchets or undulations in the landscape. In pronounced form they are often mistaken for field boundaries. In ploughing across a hill slope, soil was pushed aside and, naturally, more soil accumulated on the lower side than above. Over many years of ploughing tons of soil were pushed downhill by the plough and none, of course, was taken back up the hill. The outcome was a series of terrace-like undulations which followed the contours of a hill. Because much of this land was never ploughed again, the positive and negative lynchets still remain. Lynchets are not a product of prehistoric farming techniques only; they continued to be produced up to recent times.

Archaeologists have found many pieces of broken pottery and other household rubbish in lynchets. Thus a field may be dated fairly accurately. To the naturalist the date of a field is less important than the reason why pottery is found so widely dispersed in prehistoric fields. Animals kept in compounds near settlements produced large amounts of dung. This was collected in a heap which was also used as a dump for household rubbish, including broken pots. It is likely that this waste material was taken to the fields and used as fertiliser. Hence the potsherds found so widely dispersed in ancient fields.

Gradual forest clearances and land improvements continued through the Bronze Age and the Iron Age and, although at times fields were allowed to lie fallow for long periods to restore fertility, most cleared land remained in use, and signs of earlier agriculture were obliterated by later ploughing.

From time to time new systems of agriculture came into use. One Bronze Age phenomenon was the novel idea of enclosing large areas of land – several square kilometres – within ditches or banks. Large herds of cattle or flocks of sheep could be accommodated in this forerunner of the modern ranching system used today for beef cattle in the Great Glen of Scotland.

When the Romans came to Britain several new farming implements were introduced.

We know from excavations that the Romans used spades and hoes as well as scythes, but their greatest contribution to British agriculture was the introduction of a new type of plough which did not merely scratch the surface but was capable of turning over the sod. The Roman plough had three parts: a coulter to cut vertically into the soil, a share to slice under the sod and a mould-board to turn over the sod. Such a sophisticated plough had an instant impact upon British agriculture, since vast areas of heavy clay soils could be ploughed for the first time. So that this heavier type of plough, which was probably pulled by a team of eight oxen, could be used to best effect, the Roman fields were six times as long as they were wide, rather like the strip fields reintroduced at a later date. In small, walled vegetable plots near their houses, Roman farmers grew turnips, peas and beans. Other crops, grown in the strip fields, were flax, wheat, barley and oats. There is no evidence that Roman farmers practised any form of crop rotation or allowed land to remain fallow. From the amount of potsherds found in Roman fields we know that they probably continued the system of manuring. As well as new ploughing techniques, the Romans' other major innovation was an expansion of wool production, as a result of which Britain became an exporter of wool.

Roman methods of farming were continued by Saxon invaders, who adopted the Roman long-field system and continued to grow similar crops, so that by Norman times very little change had taken place.

After the Norman Conquest a system of common-field farming was used. Each village was surrounded by several (usually three) open fields. Each field was divided into strips of land owned by the villagers. The lord of the manor owned much of the arable land in the fields but villeins, who had to work the lord's fields, owned small parcels of land in strips. Each strip was about 10 metres wide and ran the length of the field, if possible. No one, not even the lord of the manor, could grow what he wanted in his own strips without the permission of the manorial court, which met to decide what crops should be grown in each field. Usually a system of rotation was practised, with one field lying fallow every third year. For convenience, ploughing and harvesting were done on a communal basis, with all strip owners contributing labour, oxen or both. When crops had been gathered, animals were allowed to graze. Outside the common fields were 'waste' lands and pasture available for grazing, with the village court controlling the number of animals each person was allowed to keep there.

Although enclosed field systems became more popular from about AD 1200 onwards, the old system of court leets (manorial courts) continued into the eighteenth century and, even though a farmer owned his own land, he was not at liberty to grow whatever crops he wished. From the start of the thirteenth century there was a movement away from villages, and farms were more often sited in forest clearings, where the farmer was able to construct banks, hedgerows and walls around his farm as he pleased. Many of Britain's present-day hedgerows date from this time. These are usually the type of hedgerow found at the top of a sturdy bank on which grows a wide variety of woodland plant species. Dog's mercury (*Mercurialis perennis*), bluebell (*Endymion non-scriptus*), herb paris (*Paris quadrifolia*) and wood anemone (*Anemone nemorosa*) are very slow colonisers of new hedge banks and thus, when they are found in a hedgerow, they indicate that the hedgerow was constructed in a cleared woodland site or has, at least, been in position for many years.

A more accurate method of dating hedgerows has been devised by Pollard, Moore and Hooper. They counted the numbers of shrub and tree species (excluding brambles) along one side of 30-yard (25m) lengths of unbroken, well maintained hedgerow whose age was known. They found that the average

Ancient ashes in a neglected hedge.

number of different species found in each 30-yard length was approximately equal to the age of the hedge in hundreds of years. Obviously, there are variations for parts of the country where growth conditions fluctuate from the norm.

The Statute of Merton (AD 1235) marked the beginning of enclosure – a controversial process of fencing in communal grazing land. The statute allowed a feudal lord to enclose the wasteland with the proviso that sufficient remained for the use of his tenants. So began a process which was to play an important part in shaping our landscape, a process which had its detractors right from the start. There were always conservationists in Britain who, for

Above Enclosed fields in the Yorkshire Dales.

Opposite (top) Herb paris lingers on in hedgerows many years after woodland clearance.

Opposite (bottom) Some marginal land reverts to type.

various reasons, selfish or selfless, wished to keep things as they were. The first notable conservationists were the pamphleteers of the 1450s who argued against enclosure of common lands. A later campaigner was John Clare, who wrote:

Far spread the moory ground, a level scene
Bespread with rush and one eternal green,
That never felt the rage of blundering plough,
Though centuries wreathed spring blossoms
    on its brow. . . .

He went on to compare enclosed fields with open moorlands, writing that they were:

Like mighty giants of their limbs bereft,
The sky bound wastes in mangled garbs are
    left,
Fence meeting fence in owner's little bounds
Of field and meadow, large as garden –
    grounds,
In little parcels little minds to please,
With men and flocks imprisoned, ill at ease.

Despite critics and detractors, enclosure continued apace – to the ruination of many villagers, who lost rights to their narrow strips of land. One of the leading eighteenth-century campaigners for enclosure was Arthur Young, who realised that open strip fields had to be combined into larger fields with fences (not exactly the same as enclosing the wastes) to make more economically viable units. Later, Young recognised that many peasants had suffered and he wrote: 'By nineteen out of twenty enclosure bills the poor are injured and most grossly.' They had been injured not only

Above Jethro Tull devised many agricultural machines.

Below Farming became less labour-intensive with the advent of machinery.

by the loss of strip fields but also by loss of common grazing rights. Some, who were squatters on heaths and commons, with no right to farm strip fields, lost everything as a result of enclosure.

However, Young and others like him had paved the way for modern agriculture and Britain was able to produce large stocks of grain to weather the storms of the Napoleonic Wars. This increased grain production was gained by sacrificing the interests of the small farmer whose land was best suited to the production of pigs, poultry, eggs, butter and milk. Unsuitable land had been ploughed to produce ever-increasing amounts of grain, with the inevitable result that, after the war, grain prices crashed, grain farmers were ruined and their land reverted to the rough pasture it had once been.

In 1815 the Corn Law was passed by Parliament in an attempt to improve the situation. There was a ban on imported corn until the price in Britain exceeded eighty shillings a quarter. As a result many poor people could not afford to eat bread. The only way villagers who had been dispossessed of their land rights by enclosure, or who had been bankrupted by falling grain prices, could feed their hungry families was by poaching.

Enclosure had less impact in Scotland, where, according to Scottish Law, the interest of a landlord was supreme and a tenant had few rights, so enclosure was unnecessary.

Scotland in the mid-eighteenth century was a land of subsistence agriculture, with such outmoded agricultural practices as allowing cattle to graze arable land after the harvest. On the other hand, Scotland was a major beef producer and exporter and, because of this, indirectly influenced the agricultural landscape of northern England, where a new type of enclosed field developed to accommodate temporarily the large numbers of Scottish cattle driven south from the Highlands over an intricate system of drove roads.

In many such fields cattle fairs were held.

Here the cattle were sold by auction to English farmers, who would re-fatten the animals to replace the weight lost on their long drive from Scotland. When the cattle had recovered lost weight their journey continued – to the large northern towns and cities, or to London, to provide food for ever-growing populations of industrial workers. Thousands of Scottish cattle were gathered together at fair times in large 'closes' which were situated at the junction of many drove roads. The 'Great Close' on the moor above Malham Tarn was reputed to be the largest enclosed field in the country, being over 732 acres in size and providing sufficient short-term grazing for 5,000 head of cattle. Once, the field held 20,000 cattle on the day of a sale. Nowadays, although still grazed by beef cattle, its turf is kept close-cropped by sheep and it is the habitat of the yellow mountain pansy (*Viola lutea*) and a nesting site for lapwings and curlews.

Some farms by the side of the old drovers' routes were overnight stopping places for the drovers and their herds of cattle. To advertise the fact that he was willing to accommodate cattle in transit a farmer would plant a stand of three Scots pines on a knoll or other prominent point. Small stands of Scots pine can still be seen by the sides of drove roads, indicating fields that in former times were reserved for the use of drovers.

The need to drive cattle over long distances ceased with the development of the railways – a later product of the Industrial Revolution. New ideas were not just applied to industrial techniques; they also had a major impact on the countryside, where the Agricultural Revolution resulted in greatly improved crop yields and healthier livestock.

One name associated with early farming improvements is that of Jethro Tull, who lived from 1674 to 1741. He had travelled the Continent and had seen various methods of agriculture which, he thought, could be adapted for use in Britain. Tull's first inven-

Above Breeds of cattle like this long horn (foreground) were improved by selective breeding.

Opposite (top) Primitive but simple clack mills were used to grind corn in Scotland.

Opposite (bottom) Scottish cattle, such as this Highland cow, were brought to England along the old drove roads.

Below New threshing machines processed crops more efficiently.

tion was a horse-drawn seed drill. The old broadcast technique of sowing was extremely wasteful, as we know from the biblical parable of the sower or from this old rhyme:

Sow four grains in a row,
One for the pigeon, one for the crow,
One to rot and one to grow.

Tull's new mechanised seed drill avoided such waste by planting seed in exact rows at the correct depth. Unfortunately, Tull's field workers rebelled at this new method of sowing and went on strike. Their ideas were more traditionally inspired – by the Bible. Furthermore, they were worried (rightly, as it later transpired) that mechanisation would result in fewer jobs. Tull's second invention was also mechanised – a horse-drawn hoe which was capable of penetrating further into the ground than its predecessor, the harrow. The result was the destruction of more weeds. Even at this early date our population of wild flowers was at risk.

It was Tull's belief that land need not lie

fallow if it were cultivated correctly by deep hoeing and a correct crop rotation. These ideas were developed further by a contemporary of Tull, Lord Townshend.

Townshend realised that different crops take their nourishment from different levels, or 'horizons', of the soil. Turnips take nutrients from a deeper level than the roots of grain crops, so a crop of turnips could follow a grain crop. Also, although no one knew then what nitrogen-fixing bacteria were, it was realised that land seemed to be more fertile after clover had been grown. Townshend's contribution to agriculture was the four-year Norfolk rotation, in which wheat was followed by turnips, barley and clover over a four-year period. For his efforts Lord Townshend was nicknamed 'Turnip' Townshend. He did more than merely introduce a four-year rotation, he also preached the necessity for deep ploughing, marling and drainage. His methods were almost universally employed in the south-east of England by the end of the eighteenth century and, as an indirect result, so much extra animal feed was produced that there was less need to slaughter animals before winter.

As a result of better feeding and the work of pioneer stock improvers such as Robert Bakewell, many of our native breeds of farm animals were improved to such an extent that the average weight of beef cattle sold at Smithfield Market had more than doubled between 1710 and 1795. Calves' weights had tripled and the average weight of sheep was doubled.

The progress of agriculture continued unabated, with fluctuations, throughout the nineteenth century, with major contributions made by men like Sir John Lawes. He did valuable scientific investigations into the nature of the nutrients that plants take from the soil. The Rothampsted experimental centre was established on his farm at Harpenden, with numerous small plots of land to test various techniques and fertilisers.

Lawes realised that fertilisers could be manufactured artificially and he set up a factory in London to produce superphosphate of lime and other artificial fertilisers.

As the nineteenth century progressed, more mechanisation took place on farms and fewer workers were employed. Steam ploughs, steam harvesters and threshers all deprived the agricultural labourer of his work in what had once been a labour-intensive industry. In order to accommodate larger, faster machines the progressive destruction of hedgerows began and has continued to the present day. Prairie farming techniques have to be employed in order to use combine harvesters and other large, unwieldy modern machines efficiently. Unfortunately, this has meant that large areas of arable land have been changed beyond all recognition. One should remember that these areas have undergone constant change ever since primitive man began to clear the forests. What is happening today is only a small part of the evolution of the countryside. The hedgerows we love and are in danger of losing were originally a man-made attempt to divide the countryside into manageable units. In some parts of Britain the hedgerows have, unfortunately, come to the end of their usefulness. In other areas hedgerows will continue to be used as a cheap alternative to fencing or walling. When a farmer makes changes in his use of land he is doing so not because he wishes to destroy the countryside but rather in an attempt to make a living by feeding an ever-increasing population.

When a farmer makes a decision about which crop to grow on a certain type of land he has to take certain factors into account. Assuming a suitable climate, the next consideration is the nature of the soil. Farmers and naturalists know that some plants do not grow very well on acid soils. For instance, crucifers (cabbages) thrive on basic (calcareous) soils, whereas most varieties of potato grow best in acid conditions where they are less likely to be attacked by potato scab disease. Carrots do not grow well on stony ground. It causes them to develop forked roots. Each and every crop has a particular soil requirement. Before soil test kits were invented farmers used to study the natural vegetation of a field in order to determine its condition and potential. If salad burnet (*Poterium sanguisorba*), hairy hawkbit (*Leontodon hispidus*) or other calcicoles (species inhabiting lime-rich soil) were present the farmer knew his soil could be used to grow crops which prospered in a basic soil. If tormentil (*Potentilla erecta*), heather (*Calluna vulgaris*) or other calcifuges (lime-hating plants) were thriving, this proved the soil to be acid. Other factors to be taken into account are water-retaining capacity, drainage and aeration. These depend on the texture of the soil and its physical structure.

There are many soil types to be found in various parts of Britain. These include soils composed primarily of heavy clay, sand, gravel, igneous or volcanic rocks, calcareous rocks or chalk, and peat. All suffer various problems which are determined by their nature. Over the years, by careful use of manure, fertiliser, drainage and other means, farmers improve their land and bring it up to a full potential which is still limited to some extent by the soil's origin.

One of the earliest ways of improving fertility, as we have seen, was the use of manure. Where marl (a limey clay) was available it was excavated from marl pits and spread over the surface of the fields. In limestone areas, rock was quarried and burnt with coal to produce quicklime, which was then slaked with water and spread on the fields to improve fertility (it also promoted weed growth). By the use of various natural fertilisers (including guano imported from South America) the land was made to yield heavier crops or to feed more animals. All this was at a cost because, although basic fertilisers were being used, trace elements vital to healthy plant growth were being removed

from the soil at an ever-increasing rate. In some areas these were replaced naturally by the use of seaweed, which was gathered by the cartload and ploughed in. The weed soon decomposed, leaving vital trace elements in the soil.

Fortunately, we have better methods of evaluating soil nowadays. If a modern farmer has a soil problem he needs only to phone one of the many specialist laboratories who will test and advise on the correct use of fertilisers and trace elements. Unfortunately, some fertilisers are used indiscriminately and nitrates are leached out of soil via drains and ditches into rivers, where they cause excessive weed growth.

Even if a farmer gets his soil texture and fertiliser dose correct for a spring cereal crop, his problems are still far from over. In order to get a good yield he must control quick-growing weeds which would otherwise choke a young wheat crop. In the present context we must unwillingly refer to wild flowers as weeds. A strong growth of weeds may cut crop yields by as much as 20 per cent. To the modern scientific farmer, weeds are no problem. One product recently formulated by one of our largest agricultural chemical manufacturers is claimed to kill or check most broad-leaved weeds, including 'black bindweed, charlock, cleavers, chickweed, fumitory, common hemp nettle, common poppy, corn marigold, fat-hen, fool's parsley, forget-me-not, groundsel, knotgrass, mayweeds, pale persicuria, parsley piert, red dead nettle, redshank, scarlet pimpernel, shepherd's purse, small nettle, speedwell, wild radish, field pansy, henbit, venus's looking glass, docks and thistles'.

The next problem is the control of all the rusts, mildews and various fungal infections which threaten the crop. No problem: chemicals may be mixed in, and sprayed with, herbicides. These control 'eye-spot diseases, mildew, Rhynchosporium, Septoria, net-blotch and various rusts'. Plant biologists are

Rosebay willowherb, a coloniser of neglected land.

always one step ahead in their efforts to breed new resistant high-yield crop varieties. However, the useful life of most new varieties is limited to a ten-year period, after which the disease-causing organisms produce new strains capable of attacking resistant varieties of crop. They are also capable of evolving strains which resist chemicals, so the effective life of an agricultural fungicide is also limited. Insect pests are also controlled by chemicals, but they too have the ability to develop immune strains and so new pesticide formulations have to be researched constantly.

From the foregoing it would appear that farming is a very costly business, but, if no chemicals were used, crop yields would be only a few per cent of their current values and population figures would decline accordingly. In fact, chemicals are not used as indiscriminately as is often thought. The very fact that they are expensive precludes their use except when a crop is threatened. Also, they are not sprayed deliberately on areas where no crop is growing, so there is usually a small enclave of wild flowers ready to recolonise wherever possible. Many farmers are conservation-conscious and actively manage and maintain wild areas on land unsuited to agriculture.

If all goes well and a grain crop is successfully harvested the farmer's next problem is to dispose of his surplus straw. Several methods are available but each system has good and bad points. The original method was to plough in the stubble to be rotted down by soil bacteria and slowly changed to humus and nutrients. Straw from the thresher was carted away to be sold as winter bedding on dairy and beef farms. Nowadays, because transport is expensive, surplus straw is burnt. This saves the cost of ploughing in and also saves on fertiliser costs, because extra nitrogen is needed to enable soil-borne bacteria to break down the

Traditional haystacks are still used on the island of Iona.

cellulose content of straw. If no extra nitrogen is added to ground into which straw has been ploughed a cumulative nitrogen deficiency develops with consequently reduced crop yield. Another advantage of burning is that the soil structure and the small drainage channels made by worms are not destroyed as they would be by ploughing. On the debit side, an uncontrolled fire destroys hedgerows and may kill wildlife, although most young birds and mammals are sufficiently mature to escape by the time straw-burning occurs. Insect species are most at risk and it has been calculated that about 80 per cent of a field's insect population is destroyed by burning. Insects which live in the top two inches (5cm) of soil are most at risk. Many insects are not harmful to crops and some are helpful, as they prey on harmful species.

Two new ideas give a glimmer of hope for the future. With the addition of sodium hydroxide straw can be broken down into a more digestible, nutritious food for livestock. There is also a process which compacts waste straw into solid fuel bricks.

Farmers who continue to burn straw should adhere to a few sensible rules to avoid disaster. Flush wildlife from the field first. Check wind strength and direction to avoid fires taking the wrong direction or getting out of control. Leave a fire-break between straw and hedges. The fire-break can be planted with a useful late crop such as kale or tunips, which also provides cover for pheasants and partridges.

These are just a few of the problems which cause concern to farmers and conservationists. There have been careless farmers – mainly large companies or syndicates who buy land for tax reasons or in order to get as much out of the land with as little outlay as possible. However, in 1984 the tax laws were changed in order to make the acquisition of land for tax

A weed-free crop – Perthshire.

avoidance under the business start-up scheme less lucrative. Now land should be more readily available for those who wish to farm it with a view to long-term investment for future generations. A good farmer is always very much aware that one disastrous mistake could have long-term financial and ecological implications. Conservationists and farmers have many interests in common, particularly their love of the countryside. Because we have a competent agricultural industry our population is better nourished than at any time in our history. Nietzsche said: 'When a man has eaten a little he is benevolent and reasonable.' Perhaps now is the time for a little less hostility and a little more benevolence between rival factions in the wildlife versus farming debate. As subsequent chapters will show, there are various ways in which wildlife may be conserved even on the most up-to-date, well managed farms.

2 BIRDS

Larks

Of all the birds to be found in open fields perhaps the skylark (*Alauda arvensis*) is the first true harbinger of spring, beginning to sing as soon as the days start to lengthen and the sun's rays begin to warm the ground. Larks sing most freely in spring when they establish their territories by thrusting ever upwards in slow, hovering vertical progression, all the time straining to achieve vocal superiority over their rivals. This song flight continues for up to five minutes, then the lark, probably too exhausted to continue his display, plummets quickly towards the ground, at the last moment folding his wings to land. Then he runs hurriedly towards a patch of cover. Shelley enthusiastically describes the skylark's song flight:

Higher still and higher
From the earth thou springest,
Like a cloud of fire;
The blue deep thou wingest,
And singing still dost soar, and soaring ever
    singest.

I once attended a lecture about pipits and larks, and during question time an eighty-year-old retired cotton weaver, rather hard of hearing, asked, 'What's happened to all the skylarks? I never hear any nowadays.' The question puzzled everyone, and he was assured that there were just as many skylarks as ever. What had happened was not that there had been a decline in skylark numbers but that he was no longer able to hear them. Many people think that there are fewer skylarks about purely because they go out in late spring when the birds have finished their main song period. In fact, skylark numbers have changed little over the years, although there have been local fluctuations in areas where patterns of agriculture have changed and where pesticides have been used extensively.

Some arable farmers regard skylarks as pests on the grounds that they eat sprouting beet, lettuce and peas. On the other hand, skylarks may be of real benefit, since they are voracious consumers of insect pests, rising very early in the morning to feed their hungry youngsters. According to information in an old publication about hand-rearing birds in captivity (an illegal occupation nowadays) skylark young were always the first to be active, demanding food at the first hint of dawn light.

Skylarks, because of their exuberant song, were popular cage birds in Victorian times and the cock birds were excellent singers, even in captivity. To avoid injury, bird fanciers kept larks in canvas-topped cages in case the birds forgot themselves and tried to rise skywards in song. Even in the wild, singing is always accompanied with some other energetic activity; if the bird does not fly into the air he will strut about on the ground.

Another way in which Victorians made use of skylarks was as a food. The birds were served as a delicacy in many of the best restaurants. This practice continues in some European countries and many migrant skylarks suffer. In Britain, skylarks are unmolested by either fanciers or gourmets and they are once again free to delight those who are lucky enough to see or hear them. There is no better, or more idle, way to do this than to lie on one's back in the middle of an upland pasture on a warm spring day watching the

Above A curlew's nest in a meadow.

Opposite (top) Skylark feeding young.

Opposite (bottom) Lapwings are not as abundant as they once were in arable areas.

small fluttering black specks competing with each other in a melodious singing contest.

Skylarks nest in a depression on the ground, often partly camouflaged by a tuft of grass. On average four eggs are laid, white with brownish-black speckles, and incubated for eleven days. The young stay in the nest for ten days after hatching.

Waders

Another bird of similar habitat is the peewit or lapwing (*Vanellus vanellus*). In February lapwings begin to take up their territories in fields and pastures at altitudes ranging from sea level to 2,000 metres. Lapwing distribu-

tion throughout Britain has changed somewhat over the last sixty years and the large former breeding territories of Suffolk and other highly mechanised arable areas are now almost deserted. However, lapwings have taken up new territories in north-west Scotland where, previously, they were extremely rare. Overall numbers may have changed little, although there was a massive decline as a result of severe weather conditions in 1963.

If new farming methods, and not climatic changes, have forced lapwings to change their breeding ranges it is ironical that lapwings are one of the most useful birds to farmers. In his *Handbook of British Birds* Rev. F. C. R. Jourdain states that 60 per cent of their food consists of insects harmful to agriculture. The other 40 per cent is made up of worms, molluscs, agriculturally neutral insects and small amounts of grass and cereal leaves. Worms are captured by an intriguing method. The bird patters about on the ground, imitating the sound of falling raindrops – vibrations in the earth cause worms to surface.

Unlike larks, lapwings do not require cover for their nest, which is sparsely constructed from a small amount of rushes or grass moulded in a slight depression on the ground. In the days when horses were used on the land the imprint of a horse's hoof was just the right size. Usually, four eggs, slightly pointed at one end, are laid. These are streaked and blotched on a stone-coloured ground and are very difficult to see. Peewits' eggs were, nonetheless, collected by farm workers and, when whisked into a pint of ale, were said to be a great delicacy. Until fairly recently I have seen this practice continued in the north of England. If the eggs survive for their twenty-six days of incubation the young lapwing chicks are well developed and are able to walk about and feed themselves. At this time the parents are particularly aggressive, mobbing anything that looks remotely like a predator and feigning injury if all else fails. On weekends in the Yorkshire Dales I would sometimes borrow a German setter – a wonderful dog at finding nests – as it did not differentiate between the various species of game birds and lapwings and curlews, which it pointed out with equal enthusiasm. One afternoon the dog was attacked and pecked on the head by an irate lapwing which, when its aggressive behaviour failed, proceeded to attempt to entice the dog away from its young by feigning injury, trailing one wing along the ground as if broken.

Sometimes this splendid dog would find a nest even if the parent bird was not sitting. On one occasion it found a curlew's nest, with three eggs, on a dung heap.

Normally, the curlew (Numenius arquata) finds a less exposed spot, hidden by rushes or other vegetation, in which to lay her clutch of about four eggs. Curlews' eggs, like those of the lapwing, are slightly pointed at one end and of a similar ground colour (stone to pale olive), but larger and more faintly blotched. They are incubated for about thirty days, after which the young are able to walk about within a day of drying off.

Curlews usually spend their winters in coastal regions, where their food consists of lugworms, crabs, sand hoppers and even some small fish. In inland nesting haunts their menu is mainly larvae, insects and worms.

Unlike the lapwing, which has tended to desert some of its lowland habitats, curlews have increased their population dramatically this century by colonising lowland, grazing land and rough pasture, perhaps somewhat neglecting their traditional moorland habitat, where nowadays they are less frequently seen.

With their unmistakable curved beak, bubbling song and gliding song flight curlews are, like lapwings and skylarks, true creatures of wide open spaces and a sure sign that spring is on the way.

Game

Partridges (Perdix perdix) are always associated in my mind with long winter days when the fields are bare of shelter. Then the birds may be seen standing dejectedly in small family groups or foraging for meagre pickings on snow-covered ground. Later in the year they hide unobtrusively under the cover of hedgerows and growing crops. Then they are seen only when one inadvertently stumbles into their territory or nesting site. When disturbed they fly off, making the distinct whirring wing-noise which is one of their main distinguishing features.

Common partridges (now more correctly called grey partridges) are prolific egg layers and as many as forty eggs have been found in one nest. These may have been the eggs of two or more females, since twenty is the usual upper limit for one clutch. The brownish-buff-coloured eggs are incubated for about twenty-four days and then the young are able to leave the nest just a few hours after hatching. Whenever an intruder appears near

their brood the parent partridges fly away
making a sharp, cackling 'krikrikrikri' alarm
call, whereupon the youngsters freeze and rely
upon their mottled camouflaged feathering
for protection. I am sure that this frozen
motion technique has developed over the years
as a process of natural selection. Youngsters
that do not freeze at the sound of an alarm call
would be easy prey for predators. Similar
behaviour is found amongst many other
ground-nesting species.

Common partridges and red-legged partridges (*Alectoris rufa*) are both shot as game
birds. This may be justifiable in order to
recoup something from the loss of the grain
which they eat. If grain is readily available it
constitutes about a quarter of their diet,
which consists of about six parts of vegetable
matter to four parts of animal food (including
some harmful insects).

Were it not for the sporting fraternity there

Curlew sitting on eggs.

would be no red-legged partridges in Britain.
The first successful introduction took place
in 1790, in Suffolk. From there the birds
colonised most of south-eastern and eastern
England, wherever there were dry soils. In his
1963 paper (see the Bibliography) G. Howells
linked their distribution to areas with an
annual rainfall of less than 35 inches (90cm).
These areas also happen to be the major arable
areas of Britain where pesticides have caused a
decline in insect population and a parallel
decline in red-legged partridge numbers.

Common partridges are not so conservative
in their choice of habitat and are found in
most parts of Britain except west Wales
and north-west Scotland, where either their
distribution is sparse or they are absent. Being
resident in non-arable areas, they are less likely
to be affected by chemical pollution.

Pheasants need the cover of kale or hedgerows.

The most diminutive of our game birds of open fields, the quail (*Coturnix coturnix*), is sparsely distributed, the more so as one travels north or west. Quail are small, rotund creatures, rarely seen but more frequently heard because their call is so distinctive. The sound has been likened to 'wet my lips' repeated several times.

Quail numbers have been at a low ebb since Victorian times, when they were a prized item on the menu. Mrs Beeton's cookery book contained a recipe for roasted quails and a favourite dish was quail in aspic. Quail eggs were also a prized delicacy. Many migrant quails are still shot in Europe, where quails are found often on the table but rarely in the field.

Another well-known game bird, the pheasant, prefers woodland habitats, though pheasants are often seen feeding in open fields and will nest in hedgerows. The destruction of hedgerows and small spinneys between fields does nothing to enhance the environment for many species. The farmer who wishes to conserve an ecological balance or provide cover for game birds and other species could do so by leaving small amounts of woodland at the corners of his fields where four hedgerows meet. Hedgerows are still the cheapest form of boundary and need little maintenance except a yearly cut to keep them low and dense. The main problem when cutting hedgerows mechanically is having to stop whenever there is a taller tree. This problem is solved by removing such trees from the middles of hedge-lengths but allowing them to flourish at corners, where the cutters have to be lifted in any case.

Corncrakes

One bird which does not require the protective cover of hedgerows is the corncrake (*Crex crex*). Its onomatopoeic Latin name seems to be taken directly from the song of the

Corncrake habitat – the Hebridean island of Canna.

male in the breeding season, a sound monotonous enough to qualify the bird as the world's worst singer. The disyllabic 'crex-crex' sounds rather like two cheese-graters rubbed together. What the birds lack in vocal accomplishment is more than compensated for by their dignified operatic deportment as they stand erect with head held high and beak wide open. The noise is made throughout the day in fits and starts, reaches a peak about dusk and continues through the night until dawn, when, with a bit of luck, the noise ceases and the nocturnal ornithologist at last gets some peace. I once spent a night on the island of Canna, in the Hebrides, recording corncrakes. What a relief when morning came and the raucous din stopped for a while!

I have also heard the birds in Austria but never in the fields of my native Lancashire or nearby Yorkshire, although there are occasional reports of corncrakes being heard. However, these masters of stealth and concealment are rarely seen, even in places like Northern Ireland where they are still fairly abundant. The most commonly accepted theory for their almost total disappearance from some regions is that early cropping of grass (to make silage) and mechanised haymaking practices have destroyed nests and driven corncrakes away from their old habitats. Now corncrakes are common only in areas where difficult terrain precludes the use of machinery or where traditional late haymaking takes place.

Corncrake is a misnomer – the birds rarely nest in cornfields. Their favourite nesting sites are in long grass and amongst tall weeds, often in damp places. A grass-lined hollow in the ground suffices as a nest, which may be further concealed by nearby grass drawn over the nest site as a protective curtain.

The greenish-grey mottled eggs hatch after seventeen days of incubation. For the first

Corncrakes survive only in remote areas in the British Isles.

four days after hatching the chicks are fed by their parents, then they learn rapidly to feed themselves. Flight takes place in a little over thirty days.

Corncrakes eat about four-fifths animal food and one-fifth vegetable matter. The animal part of their diet consists mainly of insects, with small amounts of slugs, snails and earthworms. Many of the insects taken are harmful to agriculture so it is a pity that corncrakes cannot exist compatibly with intensive farming methods. The vegetable content of their diet includes many weed seeds, so overall the decline in corncrake numbers has been an inestimable loss to the farming community.

Crows

The birds which most farmers regard as pests are crows, rooks, magpies and jackdaws. Even

though all four species do some damage to agriculture they have many good points as well, though few gamekeepers would agree.

Over recent years there has been much debate about our two native crows. The hooded crow (*Corvus cornix*) and the carrion crow (*Corvus corone*) were regarded as two distinct species but are now thought to be two races of the same species because they interbreed wherever their ranges meet and have produced fertile offspring. In mainland Britain, the carrion crow is the commoner of the two and has expanded its range, pushing hoodies back to an imaginary line from the Clyde to Inverness. Across the Irish Sea it is the hooded crow which predominates and there are only a few breeding records of carrion crows.

The feeding and nesting habits of both types of crow are similar, but hooded crows nest less commonly in trees because of the sparsity of woodland in the areas of Scotland which they frequent. Four to six pale-blue grey-blotched eggs are laid in a nest of twigs, lined with wool or hair, which may be situated in a tree or on a bank or cliff ledge. The eggs hatch after nineteen days and the young stay in the nest for a further five weeks.

Crows feed on a wide variety of foods, including carrion of all types. I have even seen a crow swoop in gull fashion to scavenge a dead roach from a canal. Farmers accuse them of pecking out the eyes of young lambs, but I think they pluck them out after death. However, sickly or dying lambs may be attacked. Crows will also take eggs, nestlings and older birds. For this reason they do not endear themselves to keepers, who, quite

Hooded crows replace carrion crows in north-western Scotland and are common in Ireland.

naturally, do not wish to have their stocks of game birds depleted. The day before writing these lines I saw a crow caught in a gamekeeper's trap. The trap was a large wire mesh cage over 2 metres long by about 1½ metres wide and 1½ metres high with a V-shaped roof. In a wide groove across the inverted roof apex wooden slats were set. Two centre slats were spaced wide enough apart to allow a crow to hop from them into the cage. Several stinking, bloated sheep carcases (probably casualties of the lambing season) were used as bait. This gruesome feast had attracted one crow which, having hopped down into the trap with folded wings, was caught by the simple fact that in order to escape it had to fly and, with opened wings, could not get through the aperture in the cage top. No doubt the bird would be dispatched whenever the gamekeeper arrived to check his trap. On the other hand, the captive crow's

An adult rook. Note the bald patch at the base of the bill.

alarm calls would be an effective deterrent to other crows intent on plundering game nests in that vicinity. Perhaps this was the purpose of the trap. I noticed that a supply of water had been provided and, of course, there was a prodigious supply of maggots and carrion.

It is amazingly difficult to get near enough to crows to shoot them. The wily birds soon learn to recognise a gun and, from then on, even a stick will be interpreted as a gun. When watching crows the only way to get near them is to keep moving. They have learned from experience that a moving person presents no danger. A stationary watcher could be steadying himself for a shot. Despite the fact that crows are so hated and hunted by the gamekeeping and farming communities, they have prospered to such an extent that they are one of Britain's commonest birds.

Similar hatred is also directed at the rook (*Corvus frugilegus*). Rooks can be distinguished from crows by the black 'trousers' of feathering down their flanks. Another distinguishing feature is the rook's bald patch of skin at the base of the beak. Immature birds do not have this bald spot. The beak is more pointed than that of the crow.

Rooks nest communally in rookeries, which always seem to be in a state of turmoil and strife. Perhaps the constant row and clamour is a result of the high crime rate in rook colonies, where robbery, rape and violence are common occurrences. Clumps of elms were favoured sites but, since the outbreak of Dutch elm disease, other trees have been chosen. From three to six grey-mottled greenish-blue eggs are laid. These hatch in about seventeen days. The next thirty days are crucial to the survival of the nestlings, which are most at risk from predatory man at this period. The farming community's method of killing rooks is to let off a few rounds from a twelve-bore into the nests in the hope of killing the young. However, some survive and thrive because they get all the food. When these survivors leave the nest they stand a better chance of survival because there are fewer competitors during a period when many young rooks – who are inexperienced feeders – die due to the difficulty of probing the summer-hardened ground for food. So shooting of rooks is not 100 per cent effective, and actually helps the survivors to thrive.

Rooks have always been a problem to arable farmers, who used to pay children a few pence a week to scare the birds away. Rooks greedily fill their pouches with peas, beans and cereals – the major part of their diet in arable areas. On grazing land they consume insects and worms, including many pests. Rook numbers declined in the early 1960s as a result of the use of organochlorides, but have recovered since.

Jackdaws are often seen feeding with rooks, but they do considerably less damage as three-quarters of their diet consists of animal matter. Their smaller size, silvery grey nape and distinctive 'chack-chack' call leave no doubt as to their identity. Jackdaws (*Corvus monedula*) have, by a combination of swaggering behaviour and cunning intelligence, endeared themselves to human beings much more than other members of the crow family. Consequently they are less persecuted and have moved from their traditional cliff and tree nesting sites into towns and villages, where they nest on chimneys and high buildings, with a strong preference for old churches. Like magpies, they love to decorate their nests with bright objects.

A keeper's crow trap.

A corncrake lure.

Magpies (*Pica pica*) are the pirates of the countryside and often they are as hated by ornithologists as they are by keepers because of their habit of taking eggs and young from other birds' nests. They are true omnivores and will eat anything. Rev. Jourdain records a case of a magpie attacking a donkey. Possibly this was a misinterpretation of evidence, because magpies regularly remove parasitic larvae and flies from the backs of farm stock. Magpies are particularly cunning egg thieves and will wait hours for a bird to lay an egg. Such is their liking for eggs that they have been known to steal eggs from cartons left by milkmen.

Magpies prefer to nest in bushes or in hedgerow trees. They are the most proficient nest-builders of all the crow family. The nest is made of twigs and lined with mud and a final cushion of roots and grass. It is well sheltered by a domed roof of twigs.

Owls

Barn owls (*Tyto alba*) are more closely associated with man than any other British owl. During the day they roost in hollow trees, church towers, ruined buildings, barns and haylofts. Nest sites are in similar locations. Long ago, farmers realised the value of barn owls in dealing with rats and mice. They provided the birds with nest boxes and left owl holes at the apex of barn roofs. But the

halcyon days of barn owls are over. When corn was stored on the straw in ricks, before threshing, the local rodent population benefited and multiplied. Barn owls enjoyed a period of several hundred years of prosperity until the invention of machines which harvested and threshed the grain in the field. Now there are fewer opportunities for thieving rodents and barn owls have been deprived of a major food supply. Although food is not as readily available in the neighbourhood of the farm, the owls still use farms as a base from which to forage for small rodents and birds in the surrounding countryside. After digestion, all the bones, fur and feathers of their prey are regurgitated in pellet form. By collecting pellets and dissecting them carefully in a dish of lukewarm water we can identify prey animals, which usually include shrews, mice and voles. Barn owls are at the top of a food chain and, in the days of

Barn owl

Little owl

organochloride pesticides, their population decreased alarmingly. Since the 1960s there has been some recovery and in the British Trust for Ornithology's *Atlas of Breeding Birds* (1976) their numbers are estimated at up to 9,000 pairs.

Barn owls seem to be going through a period of adaptation to new habitats and are seen more frequently in towns and villages, where they hunt in the orange glare of sodium street lamps. In the country they are best seen just as it is getting dark, or on a bright moonlit night, gliding over fields and hedgerows, pale ghosts who search soundlessly for their prey. There is nothing supernatural in their silence: it is the result of a special cushion of soft feathers on the leading edge of their wings. Stealth is required when dealing with keen-eared rodents.

Evolution has swung the balance over to the side of the predator. Barn owls are capable of hunting in light conditions where we could see nothing at all (their night vision is about one hundred times better than ours). Even in total darkness a barn owl (and most other owls) can hunt by sound location alone and the slightest scuffle made by a rodent can lead to detection and death. A cross-section of a barn owl's skull reveals about one-third brain, one-third auditory organs and one-third visual organs.

Little owls (*Athene noctua*) also seem to prefer a habitat near farms and buildings or in hedgerows. Charles Waterton first introduced little owls to Britain at Walton Park, Yorkshire, in 1842. His attempt was unsuccessful and it was not until the 1880s, when Lord Lilford introduced little owls from Holland, that breeding and expansion of range took place. Since then they have slowly expanded their range throughout most of England, north Wales and the Welsh borders, but Scotland is virtually uncolonised. I remember my excitement when I saw my first little owl perched on the shaft of an old cart. In common with most other owls, it displayed no urge to fly off. Owls are easy to watch if you are prepared to keep your

distance and little owls are usually quite reluctant to move in daytime. Since that first sighting I have seen many little owls. They are predictable in their choice of roosting places and conservative in their habits, so that, once found, it is probable that you will find them in the same place again. Niches in farm buildings are favoured resting places, as also are fence posts and tree stumps.

Little owls have suffered persecution because they were thought to take large numbers of the chicks of pheasant, partridge and domestic fowl. Although they may take very small numbers of these, the bulk of their food consists of rodents and harmful insects. Their advantages considerably outweigh their disadvantages and, like barn owls, little owls are worth encouraging. Nowadays they do not often suffer persecution although, a few years ago, my parents found one caught in an illegal pole trap.

Swallows, martins and swifts

Swallows are good weather indicators. When they arrive, from March onwards, we know that spring has also arrived. When rain threatens, swallows fly low over ponds and fields, skimming and gliding for their insect food. In warm, dry conditions insects are found higher in the air and swallows fly higher to catch them, though they hunt lower than other hirundines. What a sight when the sun picks out the iridescent blue sheen of their wings and the rufous chestnut under their beak!

Swallows (*Hirundo rustica*) fly from Africa to breed in Britain, where favoured nesting sites are usually in farm buildings, though I have seen a pair nesting inside the entrance to a mine. Usually, four or five white-ground eggs with brown marks are laid in a nest,

Opposite A swallow's nest cemented to the beam of an outbuilding.

Above House martin fledgelings

which, unlike the house martin's, is supported by a beam or rafter. Eggs are incubated by the hen for fourteen days and the young are fledged after a further twenty-one days. Swallows produce two (and occasionally three) broods. Their young are fed on a diet of insects, which are caught on the wing. Sometimes, if nesting has taken place late in the season or a third brood has been raised, swallows linger on into November.

By this time they have two problems: the rapidly dwindling supply of insects, and weather conditions over high mountain passes on their route to Africa. Some swallows have learned to avoid the worst Alpine weather by flying through recently constructed tunnels. Others have been assisted by being given passage over the mountains in airliners after

having been found exhausted to the north of the mountains. Up to (and including) the time of Gilbert White, it was thought that swallows spent their winter in hibernation in mud at the bottom of ponds. Linnaeus subscribed to this theory, which is perfectly sensible when one considers that swallows are often seen flying low over ponds in spring and autumn. Modern ringing techniques finally discredited the theory.

Swallows are at present suffering a decline in numbers. Drought conditions in areas of Africa where swallows overwinter have seriously reduced supplies of food insects. One useful way of keeping an eye on the swallow population is to check traditional nesting sites each year to record how many are used.

House martins (*Delichon urbica*) are less

dependent than swallows on farm nest sites. They prefer to cement their mud nests to the outside surface of a building, under eaves or gutters, and are frequent town and cliff dwellers. In their diet and method of catching insects they are very similar to swallows. A shorter forked tail and a white rump distinguish them from swallows.

Swifts (*Apus apus*) are faster flyers than either swallows or martins. They nest in high buildings and church towers and skim over fields and farms to catch their insect prey. Despite their speed and manoeuvrability they are occasionally caught by kestrels, the most abundant bird predators of the open countryside. Although swifts resemble swallows and martins (Hirundinidae family) in external appearance, they are members of the Apodiformes. Because of their short legs and long wings they experience some difficulty in taking off from the ground and prefer to nest in elevated situations to assist take-off.

Predators

Kestrels (*Falco tinnunculus*) suffered a decline from the mid-1950s – a result of the organochloride pesticides used intensively by farmers at the time. Since then numbers have increased despite the popular film *Kes*, which inspired many would-be falconers to take birds from nests illegally. Persecution by gamekeepers also hindered progress. One of the reasons for the recent improvement in the kestrel population is the increase of motorways in Britain, with their narrow margins of undisturbed verges where short-tailed voles (their main prey) and other small mammals thrive. These verges are the next best thing to an undisturbed meadow in some areas. (I wonder whether corncrakes will ever colonise motorway verges.)

Although kestrels are thriving at the moment, it is wise to remember that they are at the top of a food chain and could suffer again if organochlorine compounds or similar chemicals are reintroduced.

One more bird of prey, the sparrowhawk (*Accipiter nisus*), deserves a mention. Although sparrowhawks are primarily birds of woodland habitats they are frequently seen hawking amongst our hedgerows for small birds, which make up more than two-thirds of their diet. Sparrowhawks are not averse to taking occasional game chicks or young ducks and hens. For this reason they, too, have been hunted by gamekeepers and farmers. Perhaps one point in favour of sparrowhawks in the farmer's book is their partiality for wood pigeons.

Pigeons

Wood pigeons (*Columba palumbus*) breed and roost in woodland areas but spend their foraging time in open countryside, where, it is estimated, they eat their way through more than £1 million worth of cereals, peas, beans, and leaf and root crops every year. Not surprisingly, the birds are shot (there are many specialist pigeon-shooting clubs) and poisoned. Despite this persecution they manage to keep up their numbers at several million pairs. Cold winters are no disadvantage, since wood pigeons eat kale, sprouts and other winter vegetable leaves.

Several aspects of wood pigeons' breeding behaviour are unusual. They normally lay two eggs, but nests with one or three eggs are occasionally reported. These are incubated mainly by the female at night and the male by day. After seventeen days the young hatch and are fed on 'pigeon's milk'. Not exactly milk, more like a vegetable purée, this is produced in the crops of both parents. Squabs, as young pigeons are called, are weaned progressively on to a coarser mixture. Nesting is not just confined to the months from April to September but takes place at other times of the year if conditions are suitable.

Small birds

Of the many small birds which are found in fields and hedgerows space permits mention

Sparrowhawks hawk their prey amongst hedgerows.

of only a few species. The corn bunting must be included, if only for its characteristic song – like the jingling of a bunch of keys – delivered from a bush, fence post or wall.

Corn buntings (*Emberiza calandra*) frequent grain fields and, sometimes, open grassland. Their striated brown plumage is unremarkable and they may be dismissed as sparrows without a second glance. Perhaps due to use of pesticides or mechanised farming of arable land, their numbers have declined in the arable areas of the eastern part of Britain which they seem to prefer. Although their name suggests that they feed on corn this is rarely the case, weed seeds and insects being much preferred.

Finally, another bird of nondescript attire, the dunnock or hedge sparrow (*Prunella modularis*), is abundant throughout Britain. It prefers to nest in hedgerows but will use a clump of low vegetation if other sites are unsuitable. Nature produces far brighter, more

vibrant pigments than the human chemist or paintmaker can ever achieve. For me, a glimpse of a clutch of dunnock eggs is one of the finest treats the natural world can provide. Blue is supposed to be a cool colour. The dunnock proves otherwise by producing eggs of the deepest, warmest blue I have ever seen.

Equipment and study techniques

Beginners to birdwatching often ask what sort of binoculars are best. There is no specific answer; it all depends upon what weight you are prepared to carry and what price you are able to pay.

Each pair of binoculars, whatever the make, is labelled with a formula made up of two numbers, such as 8×30, 7×50, 8×40, 10×50. In each case the first number represents the binocular's magnification and the second number is the diameter of the objective, or light intake lens, in millimetres. From these two numbers you can work out a relative light number by dividing the objective diameter by the magnification and squaring the result. For a 10×50 binocular: $(\frac{50}{10})^2 = 25$.

For a 7×50 binocular the result is 49, so a 7×50 binocular should be twice as bright as a 10×50 binocular. This is only true in very poor light conditions, when the user's eye pupil is able to open up to about 7mm diameter and can use all the light provided by a 7×50 binocular which has an exit lens of $\frac{50}{7}$ or $7 \cdot 1$mm diameter. By holding a binocular at arm's length and measuring the bright disc of light in the eye lenses you may prove the truth of the statement.

In bright light the $3 \cdot 75$mm exit lenses of an 8×30 instrument project as much light into our eyes as a 7×50 binocular because our irises react to the strong light and contract our pupils. So for general use an 8×30 is perfectly adequate. Ornithologists who require more light intake and extra magnification (but with added weight) should select a 10×50 binocular. For ultimate brightness in low light, but with limited magnification, choose a 7×50 binocular.

Because our eyes are wide apart we see objects stereoscopically. Binoculars of standard type enhance stereoscopic vision (and separation of a bird from its background) because their objective lenses are set wider

Opposite Corn buntings frequent arable and grass land.

Below Dunnock and young

apart than human eyes. Roof prism binoculars give normal stereoscopic vision because their objectives are set as wide apart as the observer's eyes.

Roof prism binoculars are more difficult and complicated to manufacture so their cost is relatively high. Best value is obtained by buying binoculars of normal construction. Price has very little to do with optical excellence. The best way to choose a binocular is to go to a specialist shop and test several types before making a decision. Do not buy the first binoculars you see without comparison and do not buy one which gives double vision or eyestrain – they may be out of adjustment.

A notebook is an essential aid to memory. You may not be interested enough to note down everything you see but, if something unusual turns up, notes are worthwhile to help with identification. Your notes should include date, time, place, weather conditions (including approximate wind direction and force); then size (compare with a well-known species), markings, shape (of body, beak, legs, etc.), flight style, movement on ground (hopping, walking, running, etc.), feeding

technique, song and any other details. A sketch, however crude, is also helpful.

Try to avoid flitting about between too many areas. Familiarise yourself thoroughly with one particular district and its habitats before branching out elsewhere. Even after many years in a district you will still get some surprises and find something different each season. The BTO census of breeding birds did valuable work by allocating observers 10-kilometre squares in which to record all the species breeding during 1968–72. Observers were advised to take note of cock birds singing and displaying, in possible nesting habitats, actually nesting, and so on. Visits were made at all times of day and night. If you wish to pursue a similar project for your own interest it is wise to remember that, even after many hours in the field, you are always bound to miss a few species. Perhaps you will find them after many years of birdwatching, although it is the constant prospect of finding something different that keeps most people interested in the hobby. Finally, there is always the prospect of doing a research project into previously unrecorded aspects of behaviour.

3 INSECTS AND INVERTEBRATES

Fortunately, farmers do not have to rely totally on chemical control of insect pests. They are assisted by a legion of hungry helpers, all with a voracious appetite for insects and other farmland pests. Predators include lapwings, crows, rooks, starlings, blackbirds, thrushes, warblers, shrews, hedgehogs, reptiles and amphibians. Of course, some invertebrates predate on other species. The list of predators is endless, no doubt because insect populations are so numerous that it has been estimated that, on average, each five acres of grassland contains about a ton of insects. A similar weight may be obtained from twenty acres of arable land. Multiply this weight by the total acreage of Britain and it may be realised that we have a problem. Agriculturists fight a constant battle to protect our food supplies from destruction by insects. Insects fight back by mutating to produce pesticide-resistant strains and also by breeding prolifically whenever suitable opportunities arise.

Insects are a part of the invertebrate group named Arthropoda, which subdivides into four classes: Insecta, Arachnida (scorpions, mites, spiders and ticks), Myriapoda (centipedes and millipedes) and Crustacea (woodlice and crabs). The most numerous group are insects. It has been estimated that 86 per cent of the world's animal population are insects. However, members of all groups are found in fields and on farmland, where they fulfil their diverse roles as pests and benefactors.

Other invertebrates important in farmland ecology are Molluscs (slugs and snails), Nematodes (round-worms and eelworms) and Annelids (segmented worms).

Many invertebrates play a vital part in helping to build up soil fertility. Earthworms (*Lumbricus terrestris*) are members of the Annelids (segmented worms). They are a very primitive form of life, yet one of the most successful and necessary. Each individual is a hermaphrodite (a combination of both sexes), although cross-fertilisation commonly occurs. Eggs are laid in a protective cocoon. Newly hatched young worms are perfect miniature replicas of their parents, unlike most insects, which go through a series of metamorphoses. They are instantly ready to begin their life-long work of breaking down organic material into fertile loam and also providing valuable assistance to farmers by aerating and draining soil as a result of their subterranean delvings.

Springtails (Collembola), of which there are about three hundred species in Britain, are also of great importance to soil fertility. Turn over a pile of decaying vegetation and you are bound to find some springtails, which literally spring into the air when alarmed. Their forked tails act as catapults and have sufficient power to propel the creatures several inches. The exertions of disturbed springtails resemble a miniature aerial ballet. Springtails have weak jaws and are capable of feeding only on decay-softened vegetable matter, so they are considered to be extremely beneficial recycling agents. Professor E. B. Ford of Oxford estimated that there were 230 million springtails in every acre of soil to a depth of 9 inches (23cm). The insect world is extremely labour-intensive!

An excellent method of finding springtails is to use a Tullgren funnel (*opposite*). A handful of leaf litter or decaying vegetation is

Above Snail about to be attacked by a glow worm larva.

Right Tullgren funnel

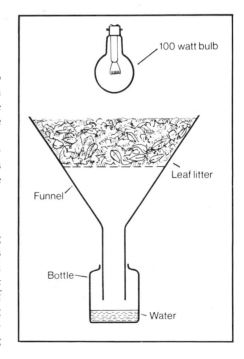

placed on a mesh grid above a funnel. On top of the grid is placed an electric lamp, which provides sufficient light and heat to drive invertebrates through the grid, down the funnel beneath, and into a collecting vessel. The animals may then be viewed under a low-power stereoscopic microscope. A hand lens of about ×6 to ×10 magnification is quite adequate if no microscope is available.

100 watt bulb

Leaf litter

Funnel

Bottle

Water

Pests of crops

The Tullgren funnel and other simple sorting methods are also likely to reveal eelworms (nematodes). Eelworms fill many ecological niches. Some are recyclers of dead organic material. Others attack various varieties of invertebrates, whilst some attack growing plants, including crops. One particular eelworm, *Ditylenchus dipsaci*, distorts growing

Banded snails on heathland, with birdseye primrose.

oat shoots and causes symptoms called 'tulip root', a bulb-like thickening at the base of the stem. Another, *Heterodera avenae*, causes root cysts (swellings) which remain in the soil until the next time oats are grown. Then more eelworms hatch out and reinfect the crop. The answer is crop rotation, but other cereals may not be grown because they act as hosts. Yet another type of cyst eelworm causes cysts on potato roots. After a crop of potatoes has been infected the cysts persist in the ground for several years until more potatoes are grown. Farmers and gardeners have found one way of removing potato eelworm cysts from soil – planting a crop of marigolds. An aromatic constituent of the marigolds, or an organic chemical similar to one found in potatoes,

triggers eelworm eggs to hatch. The resultant worms cannot colonise marigold roots so a generation is wiped out and the land is once again safe for a potato crop.

Wireworms are not worms but the larvae of *Agriotes obscurus*, commonly known as click beetles. These destructive larvae live in grassland so are most common after a field has been fallow or used as pasture for several years. Adult beetles are seen early in the year. Since they are usually nocturnal, the easiest way to find these small brown-coloured beetles is to turn over clumps of grass. Wireworm larvae attack the roots of crops, particularly in spring and autumn, so crops like winter wheat are most at risk. Sometimes large areas of wheat begin to wilt – the result of stems being severed at ground level. The larvae have strong jaws and a twelve-segmented body. Growth to maturity takes about four years so a well established community takes some eradication, although constant cultivation severely reduces the numbers of the insects.

Cutworms are likewise misnamed. They are the caterpillars of *Agrotis segetum*, the turnip moth. The moths are nocturnal, so are rarely seen. They are an insignificant buff-grey colour and their caterpillars are of a similar nondescript appearance. Many different types of root crops, including potatoes, may be attacked. Damage is rather similar to that of wireworms but cutworms tend to feed more deeply by eating down into tap-roots.

Farmers are often unaware that a crop has been invaded by pests until signs of damage begin to appear. The depredations of certain invertebrates, however, may be predicted with reasonable accuracy. Leatherjacket populations peak every few years (these are also good years for the rook population) and by watching trends closely it is possible to forecast a leatherjacket 'explosion' year and take appropriate action. Leatherjackets are the larvae of crane flies (Tipulidae family) or 'daddy-long-legs'. They feed on young growths such as seedling food crops and are an utter menace to gardener and farmer alike. Crane flies lay their black eggs in damp foliage in early autumn. Young leatherjackets hatch out in two weeks and continue feeding through the winter and spring.

Slugs also thrive in damp conditions and, like leatherjackets, are a pest of cereals and root crops. There are several types, with slightly different feeding habits. The keeled slug mainly attacks root crops whereas the field slug attacks plants at the surface. Slugs thrive in organic, humus-rich soil, which is more likely to hold moisture than a stony or sandy soil. Farmers and gardeners use metaldehyde in spray or bran-pellet form to control them. (Metaldehyde is also useful against leatherjackets.) Slugs are controlled by several species of birds, including partridges, pheasants, crows and ducks.

Shield bugs damage crops by sucking sap.

Sap-suckers may not have as drastic an effect upon plants as do the larger pests but they cause considerable long-term damage by debilitating plants, slowing their growth and reducing crop yields. Of all the many insects which feed on sap, aphids are the most abundant. They act as carriers of diseases such as potato blight. One aphid (*Aphis fabae*), the black bean aphid is sometimes known as 'black blight' by farmers. The insect has a fascinating life-cycle. There are two forms, winged and wingless, and two generations every year. Each summer, in August, winged females migrate to sterile guelder-roses or spindle-trees, where they produce wingless egg-laying females which mate with winged males. After laying their eggs the wingless females die. In spring of the next year these eggs hatch into more wingless females, which produce fertile eggs without mating. From these eggs winged blackflies hatch, ready to begin the breeding cycle over again in autumn. Several plants are attacked, but broad beans are a favourite host plant. By mid-summer the blackfly problem is naturally reduced by predation and fungal infection, so that by late summer only a few of the aphids remain to produce the next generation.

Pests of livestock

Livestock are often attacked by numerous insect and other invertebrate pests. Some of these pests cause a great deal of suffering, and even death, to their hosts. Their life-cycles and habits make interesting but gruesome reading.

Those who have read the works of James Herriot may remember the story of a farm worker who could imitate the buzzing of a warble fly (*Hypoderma bovis*), causing panic amongst a herd of steers which stampeded to the shelter of a nearby outbuilding – just where the vet wanted them for treatment. Warble flies cause cattle to stampede wildly in a futile attempt to escape egg-laying females, which deposit their yellow eggs on leg hairs. After a few days, maggots hatch out and burrow through the skin, then travel subcutaneously to the animal's back, where they settle in pus-filled cells until fully grown. They are now about one inch (2·5cm) long and cause considerable irritation to their hosts. When ready to pupate, the maggots enlarge their breathing hole, drop to the ground from their host and pupate in the ground for about six weeks before emerging as an adult warble fly. Another species (*Hypoderma lineatum*) spends some time in the gullet before moving to the back area. Warble flies must be controlled (Ministry of Agriculture Warble Fly Order 1936) whenever they appear. Derris has been used successfully but a more painful method was to squeeze out the

maggots from their cavities every ten days. Both species spoil the appearance of hides.

An even more horrific insect pest is *Oestrus ovis*, the sheep nostril fly, a close relative of the warble fly. The female nostril fly lays eggs in the nostrils of sheep. When the spiny maggots hatch they make their way upwards, via the nostrils and nasal cavities, into the sinus areas. At this stage their host's brain may be affected, causing a wobbling of the head and a dazed, staggering gait. Maggots stay in the sinuses for almost a year. They are now about one inch (2·5cm) long and ready to make their return journey back into their host's nostrils, from where they are sneezed out on to the soil for pupation. Smears of tar and creosote have been used to keep nostril flies away. These substances were also much used, mixed with rancid butter or other greases, to repel sheep maggot flies.

There are several types of green and blue sheep maggot flies. They are all carrion-feeders and, therefore, are attracted to open sores and wounds on sheep, where they lay their eggs. Another popular egg-laying site is around the region of the sheep's hindquarters, particularly where there has been a build-up of faeces in long wool. (Most farmers dock the tails of young lambs to avoid this problem.) Eggs hatch in a few hours and the maggots burrow into the flesh to feed. In a few days the maggots are fully grown and drop to the ground to pupate. Sheep maggots have a short life-cycle and are usually a transitory problem. However, in cases of massive infestation, death of the host may occur. Dipping has played an important role in the control of sheep maggots. Nowadays the same dip may be used to control the next species to be described – the sheep ked.

Melophagus ovinus is a wingless fly with strong claws to help maintain a hold on its host. The 6mm-long insect feeds on the blood of sheep and may require a day to complete its meal. Female keds incubate a single egg inside their own body. At weekly intervals a larva is

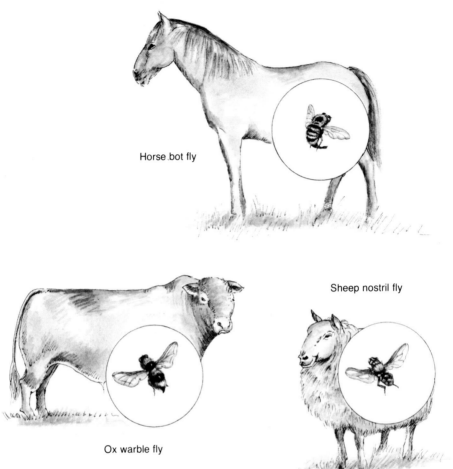

Horse bot fly

Sheep nostril fly

Ox warble fly

Livestock pests

born which pupates whilst clinging to the sheep's wool. After three weeks a new adult emerges. Each female ked may produce about twelve young but, since the life-cycle is quite short, many of the young keds are able to reproduce within the same season, thus keeping population levels high. Whenever flocks of sheep are penned in confined conditions an ideal opportunity arises for migration to other hosts.

The catalogue of insect pests of sheep would not be complete without some information about sheep scab disease. This is caused by a small mite burrowing under the skin, causing pustulation and scabbing, underneath which the mites breed and further extend their territory. The mites cause severe itching, soreness and pain in their victims. They may spread rapidly through a flock unless checked by dipping, which is compulsory in affected areas.

Horses, too, are not immune from the attentions of various insect pests. Horse bot flies (*Gasterophilus intestinalis*) are yet another relative of the warble fly but have a different lifestyle. They lay their eggs on hairs around the foreleg region or wherever the horse is likely to lick itself. (Friction, apparently, aids hatching.) Larvae travel to the mouth parts and begin to mine into the flesh beneath the horse's tongue. From there they migrate down the gullet to the stomach, hook on to the stomach lining and feed there until ready for pupation. Eventually, they are evacuated with faeces and pupate on the ground, within the pile of dung, for about a month until emergence as an adult fly.

When most people think of horse flies perhaps they have a mental picture of hot summer days spent walking near woodlands or over bracken-fringed hillsides where pestering horse flies seem to be most prevalent. Horse flies do not only attack horses but also suck blood from cattle, sheep, deer and humans. In fact, it is the females which suck blood, especially before egg-laying. Males feed on nectar from flowers. Perhaps blood supplies a much-needed boost of minerals and sustenance before the exertion of egg-laying. There are twenty-nine British species of horse fly. In some areas they are called clegs or gadflies. Females lay eggs in a patch of damp vegetation near a stream or swampy area. When the larvae hatch they follow similar habits to their mothers, preying on other larvae and on worms, which they catch and suck dry. The larvae pupate in dry soil at a depth of about an inch (2·5cm). Horse flies are most active on hot sunny days when they can make a country walk particularly unpleasant. The climates of the Scottish Highlands, North Wales and the Lake District seem to provide an ideal environment for flourishing horse fly communities. Sometimes, a spell of wet windy weather provides a welcome relief to the animals (including humans) of these areas by driving horse flies for cover. No doubt many readers use insect-repellents to avoid being eaten alive by horse flies and midges.

Midges, too, need a certain amount of dampness to complete their life-cycle. The larvae of some species are aquatic; others live under heaps of farmyard manure or clumps of rotting vegetation. There are over 150 species of midges in Britain, but there is one particularly voracious type (*Culicoides pulicaris*) which feasts upon the blood of man. *Pulicaris* larvae are aquatic, free-swimming creatures and, after hatching in late summer, overwinter in ponds and slow-flowing water ready to pupate and emerge from the water the following spring. Only the females suck our blood and the males are harmless to us. If, therefore, you wish to be selective in your efforts to protect yourself, kill only female midges. Males have branched, feathery antennae; females lack these adornments but have biting mouth parts instead.

In case you are coming to the conclusion that the British countryside is a dangerous environment populated by crop devourers, parasites and bloodsuckers, perhaps now is the time to change tack and consider some of the many insects which are beneficial to man.

Insect predators

Take, for instance, the ladybird. Ladybirds belong to the family Coccinellidae and there are over 40 species within the family. Most but not all of these small beetles have bright spots which serve as a warning to birds that the insects are unpalatable. Our commonest ladybird is *Adalia bipunctata* but, because there are several colour varieties of this species, it is often not recognised as a ladybird. Colours range from the common red with two black spots through to black with two red spots. Some ladybirds have yellow wing cases instead of red or black. The main distinguishing features of the whole family are their short club-like antennae and three-jointed feet.

Ladybird larvae are usually coloured bluish grey with pale yellow spots and are found in similar environments to their parents – on foliage, where they pursue their aphid prey. Because of the greedy way in which ladybirds hunt aphids they are very useful to farmers

and gardeners. Many rhymes have been made up about ladybirds. One, which probably originated in the Kent hopfields, is:

Ladybird, ladybird fly away home,
Your house is on fire and your children will
    burn.

The rhyme may refer to the burning of hopfields to destroy insect pests after all the hops had been picked. Are similar rhymes chanted nowadays as wheat stubble is burned?

Another useful and interesting beetle of fields and banks, particularly in calcareous areas, is the glow-worm (*Lampyris noctiluca*). Glow-worms are remarkable for producing a greenish glow by biochemical action in organs under their tail segments.

Each species of glow-worm produces a different sequence of flashes unique to its own species. (A close analogy is with the coded system of flashes which Trinity House uses for the instant identification of lighthouses.) Females glow more brightly and, in order to advertise their willingness to mate, climb up

Above A ladybird larva.

Below A ladybird hunting aphids.

The female glow-worm almost resembles her larvae.

to a prominent position on a stalk of grass. The appearance of males and females is so disparate that it is hard to realise they belong to the same species. Males are brown, beetle-like, and attain a length of about 1 centimetre. Females are a similar length, are segmented, have neither wings nor wing-cases and look rather like a smaller version of their larvae.

Glow-worms are nocturnal, hiding under stones during the day and coming out of hiding at night to feed on snails. Adults and larvae feed by similar methods. They inject a paralysing agent into a snail's body. The same injection of enzymes then proceeds to turn the snail's body into a mushy soup which is sucked out by the glow-worm, leaving nothing but an empty shell. But glow-worms don't have it all their own way. They, too, fall prey to other insects, which imitate glow-worm flash patterns to lure glow-worms to their death.

Ground beetles, members of the sub-family Carabinae (of the Carabidae), are also useful predators of many of the insect pests found in fields. They are rarely seen by day, preferring to hunt at night, tramping about on foot, hunting earthworms and various insect pests. During the day these 3cm-long glossy, metal-lic creatures may be found hiding under stones or fallen branches. If you disturb them they are likely to emit a foul-smelling substance from their anus or from their mouth. This is often their only means of defence since many species of ground beetle are unable to fly and do not have particularly powerful jaws.

Similar beetles with powerful mandibles are the tiger beetles, which belong to the same family as ground beetles but are members of a different sub-family (Cicindelinae). They are found on dry, open ground where their larvae (which have even larger mandibles than adult tiger beetles) construct burrows up to 30cm deep. At the top of the burrow the predatory larva attaches itself to its shaft by two hooked spines, then patiently waits with head and mandibles protruding slightly above ground level until suitable prey approaches the ambush. When a tasty delicacy comes within reach the tiger beetle springs into action by grabbing its prey in pincer-like mandibles, then carries it off down to the bottom of its burrow to be eaten at leisure. After a couple of summers, the larva pupates in the same burrow by sealing the top with soil. Then, the following spring, it emerges as an adult insect.

Bees, wasps and ants

The study of bees is a complex subject and much good work has been done by Karl von Frisch, who first experimented with direction-finding communication amongst colonies of honey bees (*Apis mellifera*). After a series of carefully controlled experiments, he realised that worker bees which had found a good source of nectar were able to communicate the whereabouts of their find to fellow workers by using an elaborate dance routine. If food was situated within a distance of 10 metres the finder did a round dance, gyrating backwards and forwards in complex, circular patterns. For food supplies at a greater distance a more elaborate 'tail-wagging dance' was performed. Even the scent of the flowers to be found was communicated because the upper, furry part of a bee's body retains scents for a long period of time and, also, droplets of nectar were exuded during the dance from the finder's honey stomach. By these methods it is possible for a whole hive of bees to be alerted quickly to the prospect of a new food supply as each returning worker in turn dances before her fellow workers (workers are sterile females).

Von Frisch tried many other experiments with hive bees and found that, although they may have colour perception – by virtue of the fact that different colours emit varying amounts of light – they are colour blind. However, their vision extends into ultraviolet wavelengths and many flowers have honey guides which we cannot see but which bees perceive as lines and shapes in ultraviolet light.

Honey bees are rarely found in the wild in the British Isles except when a colony has gone feral. This may happen when a new queen is about to hatch in a hive and the hive is becoming overcrowded. Then, the old queen leaves her hive in company with about half her subjects. Beekeepers await this moment, capture the swarm of bees and introduce them to a new hive. Occasionally swarms escape and may cause considerable inconvenience before they are caught. Recently a particularly vicious type of African bee has spread across the continent of South America, where they were introduced to improve apiary stocks. They hybridised but passed on their violent genes, escaped and began to attack local people. Wherever they appear swarms of ferocious stinging bees leave their hives and roam the countryside terrorising animals and humans.

Honey bees have a three-tier social system. Drones, whose job is to mate with the queen, usually die after doing their duty. Those that survive are killed by workers, which may be considered to be one rung up the social ladder, even though they have to do all the work. Workers are the cleaners, foragers, nursemaids and general dogsbodies. All are sterile females and so present no challenge to the queen. Worker larvae hatch from typical hexagonal cells and are fed on ordinary food (pollen and honey), but those larvae that are destined to be queens have extra-large, rounded cells and are fed on a more nutritious food which is often called 'royal jelly'. When a new queen hatches (in a hive which has been vacated by the old queen) she stings to death all the other royal larvae who have not yet emerged. This seemingly treacherous behaviour is necessary in order to perpetuate her genes without interference. Eventually, after three or four years of egg-laying, when she becomes too old to continue her task, she too

Bees are useful pollinators.

will be murdered by her previously faithful workers.

Man has had a long association with bees and honey has been collected for thousands of years to be used as a food or fermented to make mead. Hives have been constructed of many materials, the commonest being wood, and I have seen stone recesses for bee hives in the sides of farm buildings. These recesses were known as bee boles.

Bees are useful pollinators and for this reason their hives are often moved into orchards at blossom time. Their feeding habits vary with the seasons, beginning in April with prunus, moving on to hawthorn, apple and dandelion in May, blackberry and raspberry in June, and so on through the summer as each flower comes into season. The finest honey of the year is gathered in August, when our moorlands are ablaze with purple heather.

Honey bees are not typically bee-like in appearance and may, indeed, be confused with dull-coloured wasps. Bumble-bees (members of the genus *Bombus*) are much harder workers and better pollinators and actually look more like our accepted idea of a bee. They are usually large, furry and brightly coloured.

A queen bumble-bee mates in autumn, then hibernates until the spring, when she begins to regather her strength by feeding on nectar and pollen. Her next task is to find a suitable hole in the ground as a home for her future colony. Some species use an abandoned vole's nest which contains a ready-gathered supply of nest material. When all is ready the queen begins to fashion a spherical egg cell, using wax produced from her abdomen. Inside the cell she places pollen and several of her eggs, then seals the chamber with wax. The next cell she makes is a storage cell of honey. As her larvae develop she injects their cells with a mixture of pollen and honey. As they grow in size she builds up their cells with more wax. When the larvae are fully grown they pupate in cocoons, which they spin for themselves.

Above A wasp's nest

Left Robin's pincushion gall on dog rose.

Below Gall wasp

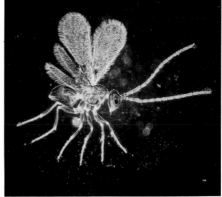

On emergence they become the first workers and the queen, at last, has some assistance in running her colony. From that time onwards she sticks to her task of producing eggs.

Later in the season, the queen begins to produce eggs which will hatch into new queens. At the same time she produces some eggs which have not been fertilised. These hatch into male larvae. Towards the end of the season all the new queens and males leave their old nest, forsaking the old queen who, by now, is in a state of advanced decrepitude. With a few surviving workers the tattered creature lives on in decadent regality until, worn out by months of egg-laying and, latterly, by invasions of parasites, she dies.

Bees, ants and wasps are members of the order Hymenoptera. Most have similar breeding cycles and complex social systems but life in an ant colony is, perhaps, most complex of all.

Have you ever stumbled over huge heaps of grassed-over soil in rough pasture land? Possibly, you thought the heaps were old mole hills. But these heaps are much larger than the usual mole hill and yet they are made by a much smaller creature, the meadow ant (*Lasius flavus*). Meadow ants are the insect equivalent of the farmer. Instead of keeping cattle they keep aphids. Many different species of aphid have been 'farmed' by various ant species. Meadow ants keep several types of root-feeding aphids which have become so dependent on the ants that they are even unable to excrete without the ants' assistance.

An aphid feeds by tapping sap from plants which, in passing through the aphid's body, is considerably changed by enzyme action and excreted as a sticky sweet substance known as honeydew. Some substances are removed from the sap by the aphid's digestive system but what remains is still a nourishing mixture of sugars, alcohols, minerals and various organic acids. This waste product of one insect is food for another and ants are able to utilise honeydew as a major item of diet.

Protein is the one main ingredient lacking.

So ants have evolved a complex relationship with aphids. In order to stimulate aphids to excrete honeydew, ants touch them around the anal region and a droplet is released.

Meadow ants not only 'farm' adult aphids but also collect their eggs and look after them like their own larvae. They inspect them constantly for mould and lick them clean until hatching, when the ants place them with their own larvae. However, the aphids soon wander off to find suitable roots to feed on. Some authorities have suggested that ants actually carry aphids to suitable feeding areas.

Although ants actively encourage aphids by providing shelter and protection from predators, wasps use aphids in an entirely different way – as food. The all-black mournful wasp (*Pemphredon lugubris*) nests in old fence posts or in dead trees, using beetle holes as nesting sites. It stocks its cells with a supply of aphids before sealing them up. Another wasp, *Mimesa equestris*, also uses a stock of aphids as food for its larvae. These wasps are often found nesting in communities, although there is no co-operation between individuals. Dry banks are a favourite nesting site. *Mimesa equestris* can be quickly distinguished by the red coloration of the basal segments of the abdomen.

Two wasps share the title 'common wasp'. These are *Vespula vulgaris* and *Vespula germanica*. They are of similar appearance, both having the familiar black and yellow stripes. They serve a useful purpose in the countryside by keeping down the fly population. Flies are caught and chewed to a pulp to be fed to the larvae.

Yet another wasp is a noteworthy predator of caterpillars. Sandwasps prepare their nests on the dry, sandy soils of heaths and downs. First they dig a hole in the ground, then they go off in search of a suitable large, juicy caterpillar. The unfortunate caterpillar is immobilised by a paralysing sting and dragged off to be buried alive in its prepared grave.

Before sealing the hole the female wasp deposits an egg on top of her victim, which will provide a source of fresh food for the hatching wasp larva. Of the two British sandwasp species, *Ammophila sabulosa* and *Ammophila pubescens*, the former seals her cells and forgets about them but the latter remembers her nest sites and, periodically, goes back to reopen the cells and supply fresh caterpillars.

Two diminutive ichneumon and chalcid flies (relatives of wasps) do sterling work in keeping down populations of cabbage white butterflies. *Apanteles glomeratus* lays eggs in caterpillars of *Pieris brassicae*. When the larvae hatch they slowly consume their host, leaving a dried out husk, before migrating to a near-by wall to pupate. *Pteromalus puparum* uses chrysalids of cabbage white butterflies as a food supply for its larvae. Although only one egg is laid per chrysalid, each egg divides and many larvae are produced so that as many as fifty or more chalcid adults may emerge from one caterpillar chrysalid.

Butterflies

Parasitic insects play a gruesome but vital role in preserving an ecological balance, though most farmers and gardeners would agree that too many cabbage white butterflies are un-desirable. There are three white butterflies: *Pieris brassicae* (large white), *Pieris rapae* (small white) and *Pieris napi* (green-veined white). All three species feed on cruciferous weeds and brassica crops, laying large patches of yellow eggs under leaves. These may be studied easily and by using a hand lens you may see some of the small caterpillars hatch out. The large white is most commonly found on brassica crops. Its greenish-yellow, black-spotted caterpillars exude a foul smell as they feed in droves on cabbage leaves. The green-veined white is a butterfly of pastures and open country. Less of a pest than the other two, its eggs are laid singly on charlock and hedge garlic.

Dark-green fritillary butterflies (*Argynnis aglaia*) frequent fields and rough pasture, where they lay their eggs on dog violets. The 'dark-green' apellation is rather confusing until you catch a glimpse of the dark green scales on the underwing area. Dark-green fritillaries are not seen on the wing until July and August because they have a late breeding cycle. Their eggs do not hatch until September, when emerging larvae eat their own egg shells before hibernating through the winter. The following April they come out of hibernation and begin to feed until June, when they pupate in a shelter of silk-bound leaves until July.

All the varieties of blue butterfly inhabit fields and downlands. Only one, the common blue, is found all over the British mainland. Other species of blues are confined to the south of England. Common blue (*Polyommatus icarus*) lay their green eggs on birdsfoot trefoil (*Lotus corniculatus*) or on rest harrow (*Ononis repens*). There are two generations in each year but, to ensure future breeding stock, second-generation larvae hibernate on the ground below their food plant, then pupate the following spring.

There are so many insect and invertebrate species that space permits the inclusion of a mere handful. Field guides are necessary for the study of each order. In the past collectors used to go out into the field with their killing jars and butterfly nets, but their methods were destructive to moth and butterfly populations. To attract butterflies and moths they 'sugared' trees with strange concoctions which often included ale, spirits and various strong flavourings mixed with sugar and water. Sugaring of posts and trees is still a useful method of attracting moths but, nowadays, collectors prefer to use mercury vapour lamps to attract the objects of their study, although this method is far more destructive than sugaring.

Far better than a collection of dead insects pinned to trays is a collection of photographs.

Opposite Common blue   **Above** Meadow brown

Below Dark green fritillary – a butterfly of heaths and meadows.

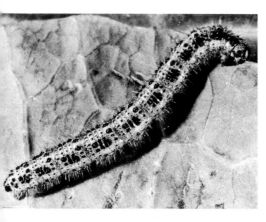

Left Cabbage white caterpillar

Below (left) Cabbage white butterfly

Below (right) The peacock butterfly is increasing in abundance in areas where insecticides are not used.

For smaller insects a macro (close-focusing) lens on a single-lens reflex camera is invaluable. For photography of butterflies and moths, where a close approach disturbs your subject, a telephoto lens of about 135mm focal length mounted on extension tubes enables close photographic approach without the necessity of close physical proximity. Try to remember, or carry a list of, various food plants for each butterfly. You are most likely to get a good photograph of a particular butterfly if you are prepared to wait near its food plant. Also, if you wish to use your garden as a photographic studio for butterflies or as a nature reserve, you must be prepared to allow some weeds to grow or even to sacrifice some of your prized plants. Many seedsmen supply wild seed mixtures so that areas of garden may be sown with plants to attract insects. If you do develop a serious interest in insects, it is unlikely that you will exhaust the subject, for in Britain alone there are 20,000 insect species.

4 PLANTS

Nutrition

Plants, like animals, need certain nutrients, without which they are unable to remain healthy. Ten elements are required for healthy plant growth. They are oxygen, hydrogen, carbon, nitrogen, phosphorus, magnesium, sulphur, iron, calcium and potassium. Also required, but in much smaller quantities, are boron, copper, zinc, molybdenum, aluminium, silicon, sodium, chlorine, cobalt and manganese. These are known as trace elements. If trace elements are present in very small quantities healthy plant growth is assured. If certain trace elements are lacking, some plants are unable to survive. On the other hand, where large quantities of a particular trace element have accumulated in soil (for example, spoil heaps of mine workings) very few plant species are able to survive the severe imbalance of minerals.

Nowadays the farming community realises the importance of maintaining a suitable balance of nutrients and trace elements. A deficiency of boron leads to root crops of poor quality and beet and turnips may be hollow-centred. A few pounds of borax to the acre is all that is required to restore a balance. Too much salt may debilitate a potato crop, but small amounts of salt are considered to enhance carrot growth. A deficiency of copper leads to poor-quality grass production. Cattle fed on such grass may become weak and spavined, and develop the characteristic spectacled appearance round their eyes as a circle of hair loses pigmentation. An instant remedy is to apply a few pounds of copper sulphate (in solution) per acre. Manganese is often applied with copper as both these elements tend to be in short supply in peat soils. Usually, soils on limestone or on chalk are able to supply the full range of nutrients. It is for this reason that the practice of liming – to release soil-borne nutrients – is a vitally important procedure if land is to produce to full potential.

Other localities where rich soils are found are river valleys and alluvial plains where regular winter flooding deposits mineral-rich silt. An ancient practice was to flood riverside meadows artificially by using an elaborate system of sluices and dams in order to divert silt-laden winter floods to enrich meadow soils. Some of these water meadows were sites for a rich variety of flowers, including extremely rare fritillaries. In nature we never get something for nothing. The lowlands

Fritillaries are restricted to old water meadows.

gain nutrients at the expense of the rain-leached uplands, where only impoverished soils remain.

The importance of lime

Far below the levels of our highest moorland, wherever there are outcrops of calcareous rocks (rocks containing lime), we may find a variety and abundance of plant species far greater than that found in any other area of Britain. Limestone rocks are formed primarily of calcium carbonate – a chemical which is easily dissolved by dilute carbonic acid obtained from rainwater and from rotting humus. Soil acidity is therefore neutralised by the presence of limestone and conditions more conducive to bacteriological action than is possible in acid-peat moorland areas result. Thus, old vegetation and humus are broken down more quickly and plant nutrients are speedily made available for new growth. When farmers spread lime on their land they are merely copying a natural phenomenon.

Basic soils are found in many areas of the country and most naturalists are but a short journey from such districts. Most notable examples are the Berkshire Downs, the North Downs and the limestones of Devon. Then there are the Cotswolds and the Craven limestones of the Yorkshire Dales and the sugar limestones of Teesdale. In Scotland there are fewer limestone outcrops but basalt, a basic igneous rock, breaks down to form a similar type of basic soil. Ireland, too, is well provided with both basalt and limestone rocks and the bleak Burren in Southern Ireland is famous throughout the world. In some of these areas the fissured, porous limestone drains so freely that soils become dry and impoverished, but in most calcareous countryside soils rich in carbonate of lime have accumulated as the rocks weathered over the centuries. Such soils are called rendzinas.

Spring gentian, Teesdale.

Above Mountain pansy (yellow variety).   **Below** Mountain pansy (purple variety).

They provide agriculture with excellent grazing land and, where climate permits, are ideal for arable farming. Except for land which overlies calcareous rock the only other situation where similar growing conditions are found are the machair heaths formed of broken shell fragments near the beaches of several Hebridean islands, where strong sea winds blow shattered shell fragments far above the high water mark.

Free-draining soils are ideal for plants able to withstand drought conditions. Some of our limestone areas reproduce conditions found at much higher altitudes in Alpine districts. A glance at a field guide will show that a species which grows in Britain at altitudes as low as 400m may be found in the Alps only above 2,000m. Our climate is able to provide similar harsh winter weather and near-drought summer conditions. A typical British Alpine species is spring gentian.

Plants of downs and upland pastures

Gentiana verna grows in short turf in several close-cropped sheep pastures on the limestones of upper Teesdale. I have never seen a truer, more intense blue than that found in this flower. A painting or photograph cannot do it justice, such is man's inability to reproduce accurately the colours of nature. Although spring gentians are reported to occur in parts of Craven, I have never been fortunate enough to find them there and have to travel to Teesdale to see them, a journey which is made all the more worthwhile by the sight of masses of multicoloured mountain pansies which grow in similar localities.

Viola lutea (*lutea* means yellow) is often found in its purple form in the more northerly regions of Britain, where it thrives in short turf overlying limestone. The purple-flowered form predominates in the sheep pastures above Alston. A little further south, in Teesdale, flowers of yellow, blue, purple, and combinations of all three colours, are

found. Further south still, in the large enclosed fields of upper Airedale (around Malham – see Chapter 1) *Viola lutea* is usually yellow in colour, with rare exceptions. Although *Viola lutea* grows in areas where the rocks are predominantly calcareous, nevertheless it is said by several field guides to frequent acid soils. What seems to be the case is that the plant thrives best in acid turf overlying limestone. In such a soil, surface leaching of lime has occurred but many of the trace elements remain from the original limestone. So it is difficult to decide whether *Viola lutea* is a calcicole or a calcifuge, but we may be sure whenever it is present that limestone also will be near at hand.

Another enigma – a plant that seems to prefer acid turfs yet is usually found above limestone – is birdseye primrose (*Primula farinosa*). *Farinosa* means 'floury' – a reference to the fact that the underside of the leaves and young stems appear to be covered in a floury substance. What a delight to find these flowers in abundance! I once had the pleasure of seeing the floor of a small quarry completely carpeted by a mass of blancmange-pink blooms of birdseye primrose. Usually, the umbel of pink, yellow-centred flowers is supported on a stalk which may be about 20cm high. Recently, in Teesdale, I was surprised to find some massive specimens growing on the edge of the Whin Sill which were three or four times the usual size. Perhaps no other British flower is so characteristically Himalayan as *Primula farinosa*, with its distinct resemblance to several species imported from China. *Primula farinosa* is abundant but local in distribution, occurring in many less accessible places. Unfortunately, other members of the primrose family have declined in numbers because they have been (and still are) picked for various purposes.

Cowslips (*Primula veris*) have been used to make wine. Imagine the number of flower heads required to make one gallon of wine

Cowslip numbers have declined in recent years.

when a typical recipe requires two quarts of cowslip flowers! And that wasn't the only use. Cowslip flowers and roots were gathered as a herb to be used in the treatment of respiratory disorders. After washing and drying they were cut finely or ground into a powder to be used as an infusion. No wonder that, in many areas, cowslips are no longer found growing in pastures or on hedge banks where they were formerly abundant. Now you are more likely to find them in more inaccessible, dangerous places such as quarry edges or railway embankments.

Primroses, too, thrive on railway embankments, where they often hybridise with cowslips to produce false oxlips (*Primula vulgaris* × *veris*) – rather like genuine oxlips but with an all-round umbel of smaller flowers, whereas true oxlips have flowers which all turn in the same direction. It would appear that primroses, because of their willingness to hybridise and their variability, are in a constant state of flux. Other species of wild flower vary slightly in character dependent on conditions but few are as changeable as primroses. Primarily to ensure cross-pollination, there are two types of primrose flower, long-styled and short-styled, otherwise known as pin-eyed and thrum-eyed. In the thrum-eyed type the flower has a long corolla tube with a ring of five stamens around the opening. In pin-eyed flowers the stamens are half way up the corolla tube and the style may be seen at the mouth of the tube. Therefore the long-tongued moths that pollinate primroses receive pollen on different parts of their sticky tongues, so that pollen from thrum-eyed flowers is deposited on the stigma of pin-eyed flowers and vice versa. Cross-breeding is thus ensured. Perhaps for this reason it has been possible to develop such a wide colour range among garden primroses, which are all descended from wild stock. Even in the wild I have seen colour varieties ranging from white through pale pink to red. Were these the result of chance cross-pollination with garden varieties or were they truly wild colour variations?

Similar colour variation is to be found in the milkworts, small hairless perennials of short-cropped turf. Common milkworts are usually blue, but white and pink flowers are often found. As well as the more showy milkworts, *Polygala vulgaris* and *Polygala calcarea* (the chalk milkwort), there are two much smaller milkworts which are so diminutive you will have to crawl about on hands and knees to find them. Possibly they are not so much rare as rarely found. The smaller of the two is Kentish milkwort (*Polygala austriaca*). Only fractionally larger is *Polygala amara* (bitter milkwort or Yorkshire

milkwort). Both have small pale slate-blue flowers, so insignificant that you will need a ×5 to ×10 hand lens to see any detail.

Orchids are among the most exotic flowers to be found on dry calcareous pastures. Capricious in their habits, they may flower in profusion one year and then, for several years, produce no blooms. Some orchids are quite common in restricted areas, but if you live in an area where they are less abundant, much careful pacing and quartering of pastures is necessary. In some of the hill meadows of the Yorkshire Dales where hay is cut so late that wild flowers have had time to seed, scented

Opposite Birdseye primrose, our most delicate primula.

Right False oxlip is a hybrid between primrose and cowslip.

Below Many colour varieties of primrose are occasionally found in the wild.

Left Common spotted orchids are found in damp meadows.

Right Spider orchid – the flower imitates the shape of a spider.

orchids (*Gymnadenia conopsea*) still grow in such profusion that the air is perfumed by their fragrance. These meadows closely resemble their Alpine counterparts in their variety of plant species. In other parts of Britain fly, spider and bee orchids thrive in thin grassland soils above porous limestone and chalk. The flower of each of these orchids imitates an insect – presumably an evolutionary adaptation to entice insects to pollinate the flower. Even to human eyes the imitations are convincing. Bee orchids are found in two varieties, the wasp orchid subspecies (*Ophrys apifera* var. *trollii*) having a point on the lip of the lower petal. If pollination is successful, large numbers of seeds are produced which are so small as to be blown considerable distances on the wind.

Grassland orchids are primarily spring and summer flowers. When the last orchids have flowered then is the time for the second round of gentians to appear. Centaury (*Centaurium erythraea*) flowers in dry, grassy places from June to September and, although it is a member of the gentian family, does not have the distinctive wide corolla tube associated with other members of the family. Much more gentian-like are the blue field gentians (*Gentianella campestris*), with several flowers branching from an upright flower stalk, and autumn gentian (*Gentianella amarella*) – a similar plant but mauve-flowered.

Plants of meadows and arable land

Moving on from predominantly calcareous

grazing land to lowland pastures and arable land we are faced with a bewildering variety of species so numerous that only a few can be mentioned in this chapter. In lowland areas land tends to command a higher price because it can be made to be more productive. Unfortunately, when land is more productive there is less chance that wild flowers will be allowed to survive. In these conditions wild flowers are classified as weeds. Even in John Clare's time this was a problem:

Each morning, now, the weeders meet
To cut the thistle from the wheat,
And ruin, in the sunny hours,
Full many a wild weed with its flowers;
Corn-poppies, that in crimson dwell,
Call'd 'headaches', from their sickly smell;
And charlocks, yellow as the sun,
That o'er the May-fields quickly run. . . .

And so the poem 'May' continues with a catalogue and description of many of the flowers which even in those days were considered a nuisance to agriculture. Of course, before the days of weedkillers, cheap labour – boys, women and girls – were employed to root out weeds. In the Yorkshire Wolds the process was known as brazocking. I am sure the word is a corruption of brassica, though whether this referred to weeding between brassica crops or to the fact that the weeds were cruciferous is unclear.

Cruciferous weeds present the farmer with one of his greatest problems because they are so quick to produce seed that they can perpetuate their species between one weeding and the next. Also, as study of plants which are able to colonise old spoil heaps has shown, crucifers are able to withstand high levels of pollution and an imbalance of trace elements. They are often the first recolonisers of land which has been sprayed with weedkillers. Even self-sown agricultural cruciferous crops are a problem. Fortunately, crucifers and brassicas have lost none of this vigour in their 'improved' agricultural varieties and are often one of the easiest seeds to germinate.

Charlock (*Sinapis arvensis*) is, arguably, the most persistent of all cruciferous weeds of arable ground. Its seeds are said to remain fertile underground for up to fifty years, ready to germinate as soon as they have been ploughed up to the surface. Although recognised as a weed, charlock has its uses and was once sold as a substitute for spinach.

Even the diminutive *Cardamine pratensis*, one of the commonest weeds of pastures, has been eaten by country people. Its leaves are said to taste rather like cabbage (I have not tried eating the plant myself). One wonders how many plants would be needed to make a meal.

Lady's smock, may flower, cuckoo flower, milk maid, to mention but a few of its names, is a familiar flower of spring. Possibly its very familiarity has earned it so many different names. To many people its flowers signify that summer is not far away.

The list of cruciferous weeds is as endless as the list of cruciferous food plants. Wherever there is a niche for a weed there is always one or other member of their ubiquitous family ready to move in. Hairy bittercress and hairy rockcress are notable colonisers of dry ground.

A much more harmful weed of dry soils, ragwort (*Senecio jacobaea*), is just as persistent as many of the crucifers. Ragwort's bright yellow multi-petalled flowers adorn pastures long after buttercups have ceased to gild the landscape. Some flowers linger into November, untouched by stock because the plant contains a substance which may cause liver damage, convulsions and staggers. And yet ragwort is not toxic to every form of life. Its leaves serve as food for the striped caterpillars of cinnabar moths and its seeds are eaten by larvae of the ragwort seed fly. Sweet nectar tempts small tortoiseshell butterflies. Even to us humans the plant is not without its uses, as a poultice for treatment of sprains and bruises.

Opposite Bee orchids thrive on calcareous heaths.

Above Common centaury, a relative of the gentians.

Below Ragwort contains poisonous alkaloids.

Poppies, too, have their medicinal uses, although one species is poisonous. John Clare called corn poppies 'headaches' (from their sickly smell). It may be that the real reason for this strange name has nothing to do with their perfume but rather more to do with confusion between two distinct species of poppy. Opium poppy heads contain morphine and have been used since Bronze Age times as a pain-killing drug. They have been grown as an economic crop in order to harvest oil from their seeds. The seeds of *Papaver somniferum* retain their viability in the ground for many years and it is a distinct possibility that the plants grew as a weed in cornfields long after their first appearance as an economic crop had been forgotten. Field workers could well have cured their headaches by munching a seed head. However, if they tried to use *Papaver rhoeas* (the common poppy of cornfields) as a similar remedy there is little doubt that they would have felt even worse. Common poppies contain poisonous alkaloids in all their parts and if present in large quantities can spoil a hay crop, though they do not grow very well in permanent meadow as they prefer disturbed arable ground. During the First World War poppies thrived to such an extent on the churned-up battlefields of Flanders that their scarlet blooms became a symbol of remembrance to the relatives and comrades of the soldiers who had fallen in battle. However, not all common poppies are red and it is a useful botanical exercise to note some of the variations which occur in an area where poppies are widespread. There are white, pink and banded flowers. The Reverend W. Wilks was so interested in their variability that he decided to collect seeds from some of the more exotic variants. Then, by a process of selective breeding, he established the beautiful culti-vated strains of Shirley poppies which add such bold splashes of vivid colour to many cottage gardens. Nowadays cornfields are so tidy and weed-free that poppies are found only in neglected corners where weedkiller sprays

have failed to penetrate. But the seeds are viable for up to eighty years and if some farmer, lulled into a false sense of security, neglects his spraying, then for one brief summer a field of poppies may be reborn in all its former glory and the vibrant gold and scarlet colour scheme, nowadays rarely seen except in Victorian landscape paintings, once more enhances the harvest scene.

To some extent, poppies have managed to hang on in their old habitats, though in drastically reduced numbers. The same cannot be said for cornflowers and corn marigolds. Corn marigolds prospered in disturbed ground before the advent of weedkiller chemi-cals and mechanical harvesting techniques. Now, like the corncrake, they have been virtually eliminated from their old habitats and banished to the outer edges of their realm – to the sandy soils of Northern Ireland, the north-west Highlands of Scotland and some of the Hebridean islands – where smaller, stunted versions of their original southern England relatives still survive.

Several other members of the daisy family (which includes dandelions) may be and often are classified as weeds. Yet they are not poisonous to humans or cattle and have been used as crop plants in the past. Perhaps the dandelion is the most widespread of all wild flowers. Pasture land and meadow land may contain such an abundant dandelion crop that from a distance it appears to be an unbroken patch of blazing yellow. Dandelion leaves have been cultivated as a useful salad crop. Blanched, by covering with an inverted plant pot, their taste is less astringent than that of older, darker leaves. Dandelions exude a white, milky latex-like substance when cut. The roots, which resemble thin carrots, have been used in wartime as a coffee substitute. Roasted and ground, then infused in the normal way, they make an insipid caffeine-free coffee.

A much more tasty coffee is made by using the tap-roots of chicory – a tall blue-flowered cash crop which often lingers on as a weed many years after chicory as a crop has ceased to be grown. The taste of chicory is slightly bitter, but it makes an excellent additive to coffee and, personally, I prefer the taste of coffee with chicory. It is doubtful whether chicory was originally a native plant. Many other plants which we take for granted as being British natives may, in fact, have been introduced. Chicory still survives around the borders of cornfields.

Even red clover, the abundant improver of meadow land, is a possible introduction to Britain, though most botanists regard it as a native species. Clovers are marvellous utility plants without which no grassland is complete. Whenever reseeding of a meadow takes place it is common practice to include clover seed with the grass-seed mixture. There are several important reasons for this. First, clover root nodules contain nitrogen-fixing bacteria. Secondly, because it is able to take advantage of this extra nitrogen source, clover foliage contains more protein than most grasses. Thirdly, extra nitrogen is available in soil to enhance grass production. Finally, some clovers absorb more minerals from soil than grasses. White clover (*Trifolium repens*) is a particularly good source of calcium and magnesium. Thus clovers are a good natural method of avoiding mineral deficiency in cattle and sheep.

Clover varieties may be obtained, tailor-made, to suit different growing conditions. There are several varieties of red clover (*Trifolium pratense*), all with different flowering periods. Early clovers are less persistent and are best used for a single season. Later-flowering varieties of red clover may be sown in established grassland and persist for several years of silage or haymaking. In the long run, improved varieties revert to type.

White clover is a smaller plant which sends out free-rooting runners. It is a useful plant for grazing pastures, helping to maintain a close-knit sward. Other useful fodder crops are lucerne and sainfoin, which were introduced from Europe. Look out for a newly introduced fodder crop with nitrogen-fixing nodules on its roots. Before long, fields in the south of England will be purple with lupin blooms, a new type of lupin having been bred specifically for agriculture.

Several plants linger on as weeds after outliving their usefulness as agricultural crops. Some species of comfrey were introduced to Britain to be grown as green manures and cattle food. That is, they were grown to maturity, then ploughed into the ground. *Symphytum orientale* and *Symphytum peregrinum* have both masqueraded under the name of Russian comfrey. Although they are not grown economically at present, they still survive as wild plants. They are often mistaken for our native common comfrey, but the leaves of *Symphytum officinale* are broader and more bristly than those of Russian comfrey. Country people gave the plant the name of 'knitbone' because its roots could be made into a paste which set hard and, like plaster of Paris, could be used to set bones. Comfrey leaves have been used to poultice wounds and I remember hearing the story of a Lake District trail hound whose leg, lacerated beyond repair by a barbed-wire fence, was bound in comfrey leaves and miraculously healed. Tea made from dried comfrey leaves, taken regularly, was said to alleviate arthritic symptoms, though recent research has shown comfrey to be carcinogenic if taken internally.

Grasses

Before farming became a scientific industry little thought was given to the type of grass to be grown in a particular situation. Usually, it was thought that whatever grew naturally was best encouraged and reseeding with a new variety was best avoided. However, many new strains of grass have been evolved by plant breeders from traditional varieties. It is unnecessary for the amateur botanist to be

Above Poppies were once the most abundant flowers of cornfields.

Left Russian comfrey was grown as green manure.

able to recognise all the various strains of a particular species, but some knowledge of the wild grasses from which they have evolved is invaluable since most artificially bred grasses eventually revert to the wild type.

One of the most nutritious grasses for cattle is common rye-grass (*Lolium perenne*), an extremely variable perennial – probably the first grass to be cultivated, being first sown in Britain in the seventeenth century. Rye-grass is easily recognised by the flattened flower spikelets arranged alternately on either side of the stem, occasionally clustered together, though usually quite far apart.

Cocksfoot (*Dactylis glomerata*) grows well on poor, light soils. Its coarse blue-green foliage produces masses of fodder of a lower

Common rye grass

Cocksfoot grass

Common
cat's-tail grass

Meadow grasses

nutritional value than rye-grass. On land which is undergrazed cocksfoot tends to form thick tufts of almost inedible vegetation. Farmers need to ensure that the grass is grazed in early spring in order to avoid later coarseness and tufting. The plant's distinctive name arises from the arrangement of flowering tufts which spread like a cock's foot.

One of the commonest of all meadow grasses, possibly the meadow grass *par excellence*, is timothy (*Phleum pratense*), which thrives best in heavier loamy soils and has a long productive season, even remaining green in winter. Timothy is easily recognised by its blue-green foliage and cat's-tail seeding heads or panicles. In fact, the country name used to be cat's-tail grass until an American, Mr Timothy Hanson, took seed from New York State to Carolina, where he introduced the plant as 'Herd-grass'. Timothy is often grown and sown in company with meadow fescue (*Festuca pratensis*), a plant with tall stems and loosely arranged panicles which thrives best in rich, damp soils.

Many other species of grass are utilised by farmers. All need careful management and correct use of organic and inorganic fertilisers and manures to promote good growth. For years, country people have complained about the scarcity of their mushroom crops, blaming the loss on the disappearance of horses and the increasing use of chemical fertilisers. Horse manure was said to be good for mushrooms, although it is difficult to understand why cow manure should not give similar results.

Fungi

Recently, we have had an excellent mushroom autumn and the old myths about the relationship between horses and mushrooms have been exploded. Mushrooms thrive in a moist, humid autumn after a hot, dry summer. Weather conditions seem to pass through mini-cycles and the recent decline of mushrooms may be attributed to a series of cold, wet summers throughout the seventies. But 1983 was a magnificent exception and pastures were whitewashed with masses of tasty fungi. One village store I know had been selling cultivated mushrooms at the usual high prices. Last autumn their prices began to creep down and down every day until in the end there was a notice on the counter which proclaimed 'Free mushrooms, take as many as you want!'

All the local farmers and villagers were suffering from such a surfeit of mushrooms that they, helpfully, decided to take them to the shop to be given away. Mushrooms were bottled, dried and frozen. They were eaten with every meal of the day, souped, fried and casseroled, and raw in salads – until there was a period of cooler weather and a sudden end to the supply.

Mushrooms may be found quite easily in short turf but often they are abundant, though difficult to find, in longer meadow grass. Field mushrooms (*Agaricus campestris*) may be confused with several poisonous species which grow in similar conditions. A field mushroom should have pink gills (later brown) and a creamy white cap. If you find mushrooms with white gills, or gills which develop a yellow or pink stain when cut, do not eat them. There are several indigestible mushrooms with white gills but the blusher (*Amanita rubescens*) and yellow-stainer (*Agaricus xanthoderma*) can cause severe stomach upsets. A larger relative of the field mushroom, the horse mushroom, has a stronger and, to my mind, better flavour. A good horse mushroom specimen may measure up to 30cm across and can provide a meal for several people. And, still on the subject of edible fungi, you may be fortunate enough to find a giant puffball, a pale, football-sized fungus (not to be confused with smaller, poisonous, earthballs). Roasted whole in a roasting tray in the oven, covered with strips of bacon fat, then carved like a joint of meat, puffballs make an unusual meal.

But you don't have to eat something to enjoy it. Many of the beautiful fungi found in pastures are either tasteless or mildly poisonous, but most fungi are worth a closer look. Many, like scarlet hood (*Hygrophorus coccineus*) and *Hygrophorus obrusseus*, have vividly coloured caps. It is also interesting to look closely at their gills with a low-power microscope or a high-power hand lens to see the masses of spores waiting to be disgorged into the atmosphere.

Plants of hedge banks

Every field has its boundaries and the various ways in which boundaries are marked provide us with millions of ribbon-shaped nature reserves where sprays and chemicals are less frequently used. It is along hedge banks, walls and fence sides that some of our most familiar wild plants are still found. Many hedgerow species have a rich variety of names in local folklore. This is no accident, as the old methods of travel were slow and tedious and most country people travelled the lanes on foot. There was plenty of time to look at wild flowers and to christen them with fanciful names or to make up stories about them.

Arum maculatum grows by hedges as far north as southern Scotland, preferring calcareous soils. The plant has many names – lords and ladies, cuckoo pint, wild arum, wake-robin and Jack-in-the-pulpit are common variations. The name Jack-in-the-pulpit refers to the imagined similarity between the flower and a preacher in his pulpit. The brown or purple spadix represents the preacher and the pale green sheathing spathe is his pulpit. Cuckoo pint is one of the first plants to begin a new season's growth, its arrow-shaped leaves often appearing above ground in January before there is any competition between plants for weak spring sunlight. The flower cannot be said to be colourful or attractive, but pollinating insects are attracted by its foetid scent. If pollination is successful a cluster of flame-red berries is produced in autumn.

Another well known 'Jack' is Jack-by-the-hedge or garlic mustard (*Alliaria petiolata*). A member of the prolific crucifer family, garlic mustard has heart-shaped leaves which smell weakly of garlic when crushed. This does not deter the caterpillars of green-veined white butterflies from feeding upon it. The plant has also been eaten by humans, as one of its names, poor man's oatmeal, suggests. Its leaves may be eaten whole, in salads, or finely chopped and served as a garnish on lamb.

Umbellifers appreciate the slightly sheltered environment afforded by walls and hedgerows. Cow parsley, hedge parsley and hogweed are common. Giant hogweed (*Heracleum sphondylium*) is an interloper from Asia but has become naturalised by hedgerows and ditches. Its hollow stems look like ideal blowpipes and pea-shooters for children, but woe betide the child who puts his lips to the plant or even handles the stems. Small hairs contain an irritant poison capable of causing painfully severe skin rashes. Our alarmist press has not been slow to realise the newsworthiness of

Yellow spathed arum

such a potentially sinister plant. There have been many scaremongering stories and even demands for the total extinction of a plant which has been compared with John Wyndham's malevolent triffid.

A more pleasant member of the umbellifer family, sweet cicely (*Myrrhis odorata*), may be used as an aniseed flavouring. Its crushed leaves are mildly fragrant, but the seeds contain an oil which smells more strongly of aniseed. The umbellifer family contains many useful plants. Some have been 'improved' to give us parsnips, carrots and celery. Others, such as hemlock, are beyond improvement but, still, are appreciated by writers of murder stories. To study umbellifers a good field

Opposite (top) *Coprinus micaceus* grows in meadows on the stumps of old trees.

Opposite (bottom) Giant puff balls, the size of a football, may be roasted and eaten.

Right Cuckoo pint berries in autumn.

Below Cuckoo pint is one of the first plants to produce new leaves in early spring.

Giant hogweed, introduced from Russia.

our most numerous cranesbills is herb robert (*G. robertianum*), with small pink flowers and feathery leaves borne on rambling stems. Herb robert is replaced in limestone walls by shining cranesbill (*G. lucidium*), so named because its leaves are hairless and glossy.

Walls also provide a variety of habitats, depending on aspect and situation, for many species of flowerless plants – ferns, mosses, liverworts and lichens. Most flowerless plants appear drab and uninteresting until viewed under a magnifying glass. Some are used as dyes, foods or food additives and as medicines. Lichens, some of which contain antibiotics, are useful indicators of pollution and are the first plants to die in a polluted environment. Perhaps the reason for this is that lichens are in reality two plants, an alga and a fungus, living in a symbiotic relationship so that neither could live without the other.

One interesting exercise is to identify and catalogue the lichen species of your own locality, then repeat the exercise in another part of the country. Most western areas enjoy clean air which has been purified by thousands of miles of Atlantic Ocean. So it is usually in these western areas that the greatest variety of lichen species occur.

Study methods

When studying plants our most invaluable accessory is a notebook and pencil with which to note down details of any species difficult to identify. Notes should include all the information that is usually found in a field guide. The following are the most important details: (a) soil type and condition; (b) position and aspect; (c) height and shape of plant; (d) annual or perennial; (e) downy, hairy or not; (f) colour and shape of flowers, including information about stamens, styles, sepals, petals, etc.; (g) how flowers are carried; (h) fruit shape and colour; (i) shape, length and arrangement of leaves; (j) abundance of plant; (k) any other details, for example whether there are larvae feeding on

guide with a comprehensive key comparing leaves and flowers is required. Often, the mature seed heads are the most distinctive feature of umbellifers.

Members of the cranesbill family (Geraniaceae) are identified by the shape of their seeds, since all cranesbills have beaked fruit – hence their name. Meadow cranesbill (*Geranium pratense*) is rarely found in any but old-fashioned meadows and even then only in the remoter parts of Britain. Its usual habitat is by roadsides and on hedge banks, where it replaces the earlier-flowering wood cranesbill in succession. Meadow cranesbill flowers are pure sky-blue, whereas wood cranesbill has a more reddish mauve-tinged flower. One of plant, or whether galls or diseases are present.

It is useful to carry a field guide with you, but if you are interested in a wide variety of fauna and flora you may need a travelling library to give you all the information you want. So the next best thing is to take notes.

It is illegal to pick flowers and the philosophy of 'Well I'm just going to take one flower for identification' will not do nowadays. Nor is it legal to uproot flowers, even if you do intend to grow them in your garden. Some of our rare wild flowers have been pushed to the verge of extinction by this practice. In any case, it is highly unlikely that your garden would provide the right environment for a species which is rare, since rare plants need specialised conditions to survive. If you wish to grow wild flowers in your garden, many seed firms now have an extensive range of native wild flowers in their catalogues. A few years ago I was fortunate enough to see the extremely rare lady's slipper orchid (*Cypripedium calceolus*) growing in the wild. I cannot divulge its location (nor would I wish to), as I had to sign a declaration undertaking not to reveal its whereabouts. A Department of the Environment warden was on duty throughout the flowering season and, as he conducted me through a maze of trip wires and electronic warning devices, he showed me the empty hollows from which several orchids had been stolen by plant thieves who cared nothing for the pleasure of others or for the continued existence of such a rare plant. I was able to photograph the orchid and thereby gained a much more lasting souvenir than if I had uprooted the plant or picked a flower.

For plant photography a single-lens reflex camera is ideal. Using a standard lens on an extension tube or a macro lens of about 50mm focal length it is possible to take satisfactory close-ups of flowers. A fine-grain colour transparency film of medium speed is essential. Natural lighting is usually better than flash, which should be used only in dull light conditions and if all else fails. Yellow, pink and red flowers often reproduce best if they are photographed in sunlight that is not too contrasty. However, blue flowers are the bane of the photographer's life and often come out pink if they are photographed in sunlight, since blue and red flower pigments are of similar chemical composition. So try to photograph blue flowers in shade to get really accurate colour. Also, in order to get an accurate exposure, it is better to use an off-the-camera incident light meter with diffusing cone, then add on exposure if using an extension tube according to the information supplied with the tube. If you wish to use a built-in meter, exposure adjustments may be necessary to compensate for the fact that a green background of foliage reflects very little light and fools an automatic camera into over-exposing a flower close-up. So, for automatic cameras with no manual override, try setting the film speed at double its actual value when photographing flowers in a predominantly green background. When using a built-in meter with manual setting, try the same technique or close down the lens by one stop, for example from f5·6 to f8. Remember, the higher the f number, the greater the depth of field.

Once your collection of plant photographs attains a certain size it is a useful exercise to subdivide it into sections such as mountain flowers, dune plants, fungi etc. Perhaps this will lead to an interest in a particular aspect of plant life. You can, for instance, research the variation of a species due to different growing conditions and a library-based project could be the study of plant drugs. It is not beyond the realms of probability that new types of agriculturally or horticulturally useful plants could be produced by a process of selective breeding from wild seeds. Some seedsmen offer prizes to anyone who can introduce a new variety of plant to horticulture. Every plant grown by farmers and gardeners was originally developed from a wild species.

Right Lady's slipper orchid, arguably our rarest wild flower.

Below Meadow cranesbill.

5 TREES AND SHRUBS

Although many of our hedgerows date from the era of parliamentary enclosure, many others are hundreds of years older. Illustrations exist of thirteenth-century hedges, and it is quite possible that hedges were used as stock enclosures even before the thirteenth century – though whether the hedges were planned or grew naturally or were survivals of woodland is uncertain.

Originally, field boundaries were marked by ditches and banks, the bank being made of earth excavated from the ditch. Obviously these were not sufficiently stock-proof to contain the more athletic varieties of domesticated animals, so the practice of hedging was developed and bushes were grown on top of the banks. Probably, the first hedges were what are known as 'dead hedges' and were constructed of miscellaneous dead scrub gathered from nearby woodland – a type of hedge that may have existed in primitive form as long ago as the Stone Age, when cave dwellers blocked their cave entrances with brushwood to keep out wild animals. Later, dead hedges were made of coppiced wood and eventually developed into wickets or hurdles of interwoven, pliable hazel twigs, and were used as temporary stock enclosures.

But dead hedges are today of little importance, perpetuated mainly by contests at agricultural shows and the famous annual ceremony at Whitby, where a hurdle has to be constructed sturdy enough to withstand the force of three tides.

Living hedges are much less fragile and are still a cheap form of stock enclosure if they are planted correctly and maintained regularly. Regular maintenance over centuries has pre-served many antique hedges, which may be dated by the number of shrub species which they contain (see Chapter 1). It is common practice to plant a hedge with one species of shrub – and if a mixed hedge is planted, it is unlikely that more than a single species will thrive. This is because hedges have to be planted very densely. Generally, spacing of 15–30cm is recommended and the preferred distance for hawthorn is 22cm. An interloper is therefore unlikely to survive overcrowding by a dominant species, although eventually other species are able to take over when large gaps occur. Various species are used in different parts of Britain, but hawthorn seems to be preferred. Beech is popular in restricted areas, including parts of southern England and southern Scotland, where it grows thickly enough but lacks the deterrent thorns of blackthorn and hawthorn. Elder is a common hedgerow tree, but is usually bird-sown rather than planted by farmers and it is easily pushed aside by wandering animals. Ash, elm and hazel hedges were probably originally planted as a dual purpose hedge that could also be coppiced (cut down almost to ground level every ten years) to provide strong straight poles for hurdle-making. Willows served a similar purpose but were more often pollarded a few feet above ground level.

Close planting aids quick upward and outward growth, speeding up production of a dense hedge, even if a number of trees fail to grow. It is difficult to avoid some gaps in a new hedge, but species such as elm quickly throw up suckers to fill the gaps. Replanting of small gaps, even with trees of the same species, is rarely successful because established

trees take all the soil nutrients and light.

Various methods are used to keep hedges in tidy, dense condition. The modern method of hedge clipping by motorised equipment precludes the growth of the tall hedgerow trees which were once a common sight in the countryside. However, machine-hedging is quick and easy and, if carried out regularly (every year in some cases), a dense hedge is the result, though only in the case of thorn hedges. With other species the hedge grows progressively thinner at ground level and ceases to be stockproof. In mixed hedges this leads to farmers having to cobble up their fences with unsightly lengths of timber and wire. What they really should do is weed out all but thorns and attempt to replant large gaps with more thorns so that the hedge may be successfully machine-trimmed in the future, even though that leaves it devoid of variety. Until mechanised trimmers were used hedges were layered – an effective management technique for all hedge species, although (as mentioned earlier) some, such as hazel and ash, could be coppiced to provide a supply of straight posts or even to provide firewood. When layering took place the hedge tops were trimmed down and main trunks were chopped nearly through, then bent and layered almost horizontally along the fence line. Pegs cut from waste timber were used to hold layered material firmly in place. New season's growth would sprout upwards from the old stumps and the layered branches, even though they might appear to have been severed beyond regrowth. At the next layering, previously layered branches were hacked out and new vertical growth was layered to take the place of the old ensuring vigorous growth.

In some parts of the country a method which required less expertise was used. Here, double hedges were planted with a narrow gap between. Every eight years one hedge was coppiced to ground level; the other then acted as a fence until its twin recovered. These double hedges were superb wildlife refuges where badgers could make their sets in absolute secrecy.

As well as containing stock, hedges have long been used to mark boundaries. By looking at an old boundary hedge on a bank by a ditch it is possible to decide who was responsible for maintenance of the hedge and who owned the land. Almost invariably it was the farmer on the bank side who owned the bank, the hedge and the ditch, the farmer on the ditched side owning land only up to the ditch line.

Advantages of hedgerows

Recently it has been found that hedges are excellent filters of atmospheric pollutants. Along the sides of busy trunk roads, where an incessant stream of traffic pours out a poisonous mixture of soot, lead, sulphur dioxide, carbon monoxide and carbon dioxide, evergreen trees and shrubs have great difficulty in surviving because their leaf pores (stomata) become clogged with soot. Deciduous hedges do not appear to be inhibited by roadside conditions as they grow a new set of leaves every year which do not have time to become thickly coated with soot before they are shed. A good dense hedge by a road also acts as a buffer to stop lead reaching grass and crops. Animals feeding on grass next to an open wire fence by a roadside are more likely to absorb harmful amounts of lead than animals which feed on grass behind a roadside hedge and vegetables, fruit and grain, too, are better protected by a thick hedge. Fortunately, the dangers of lead pollution have at last been realised and lead as an anti-knock device in petrol is about to be gradually phased out over a period of years. Since hedgerow trees are such efficient absorbers of lead, it is obvious that elderberries, blackberries and

Opposite Traditional hedging practices have given way to mechanised hedge trimmers.

other fruits gathered by a busy road may contain small amounts of the toxic metal and are best left alone.

Hedges are of indisputable value as shelter from wind and weather for all manner of farm stock and as a refuge, feeding area and breeding territory for many forms of wildlife. For this reason alone they are worth preserving. Now that hedgerows are threatened in many parts of the country it is vital that naturalists, farmers and the public in general should understand their value and do their utmost to save them – and even plant more where circumstances permit. After all, they are the cheapest form of fencing if managed correctly.

In the RSPB survey *Farming and Wildlife* several important facts about hedges were revealed. It seems that the best hedges for wildlife are tall and unkempt with good ground cover untouched by weedkillers at the base, though such a hedge often has gaps through which sheep may stray. A well maintained hedge has an A-shaped cross-section and a height of about 1·5 metres – and also a distinct lack of wildlife.

The survey also revealed, not surprisingly, that older hedgerows contain the richest variety of plant species. It is therefore important that these hedges should benefit from more sympathetic management – for example, by omitting the annual burning and spraying of hedge bottoms, which provide excellent nesting sites for partridges, pheasants and many smaller birds.

Another bonus of the retention of hedges is their deterrent value in preventing trespass into growing crops and also their usefulness as path indicators (most paths follow a hedge or bank line). The survey's final recommendation was to do all hedge trimming in autumn and winter, thereby avoiding damage to nest sites. If hedges are trimmed on a two- or three-year cycle shrubs are able to bear berries as a winter food supply for wildlife.

Victim of Dutch elm disease – the remains of a hedgerow elm.

Elm

Elms are, perhaps, the commonest trees of farmland and are often found standing alone in the middle of fields or as hedgerow trees. In old relic hedges the elms are probably surviving remnants of forest-edge trees whose roots threw up suckers along the hedgerow. English elms (*Ulmus procera*) were once a familiar sight in our fields and hedgerows – until Dutch elm disease began to run its course like a selective forest fire across the land, leaving nothing but decayed and gnarled skeletons as a reminder of what had been. Many birds, in particular rooks, lost valuable nest sites and farm stock were deprived of

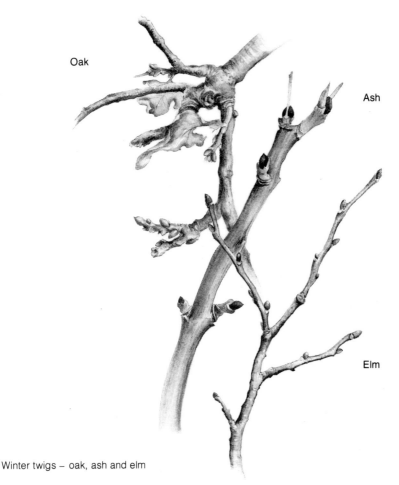

Oak

Ash

Elm

Winter twigs – oak, ash and elm

much-needed summer shade. There was a time when scientists thought the disease was most virulent in English elm and that the seven or so other species of elm found in Britain (including wych elm) were immune. It is now known that this is not the case and all species are threatened.

Traces of Dutch elm disease have been noticed since the early nineteenth century but this original strain seems to have been less damaging and most trees survived its attack. Signs of the disease have been found in wooden items dating back to that time. The disease-causing organism is a fungus,

Ceratocystis ulmi, which triggers (belatedly) an automatic immune system in an infected elm. In order to avoid further spread of fungal infection, the vessels which carry water up the trunk to the leaves are blocked by swellings. Leaves yellow, die and are shed, then the whole tree becomes infected and, finally, is left as a gaunt unclothed framework.

Some trees were able to survive, particularly in wet summers, but in years of drought the elm population suffered the highest numbers of losses. Recently, however, a more virulent mutation of the fungus has developed and few trees are spared.

Elms are often reproduced by suckering from roots. Thus an entire local population may be interconnected and once one tree is diseased surrounding clones soon succumb. Why should a fungus spread so easily from area to area? The answer is that the European elm bark beetle (*Scolytus scolytus*) acts as a carrier. Without this flying delivery service Dutch elm disease would be no problem. With the help of the elm bark beetle the fungus spreads rapidly. The beetles produce two generations each year, one in spring and another in late summer. Eggs are laid in a chamber under elm bark. When the larvae hatch they eat their way through the sapwood, making rambling excavations under the bark. As they proceed through a fungus-infected tree some fungus must be eaten by the beetles and absorbed, and the spores are retained within the pupating larvae. When adult beetles emerge they carry away with them the deadly spores to infect another elm. Various treatments have been tried. Some control the beetle, others control the fungus, but all have failed – usually because the cost was too great or the task too formidable. There is, however, some hope for the future. Forestry Commission scientists have isolated a virus which attacks the fungus. It is a naturally occurring virus and wherever it occurs the Dutch elm fungus is considerably weakened and most trees survive. The problem now is how to get the virus to spread. Could the elm bark beetle act as a vector for both fungus and virus? Another ray of hope is the inability of the elm bark beetle to survive cold winters. Therefore Dutch elm disease is slow to spread northwards and may never reach parts of Scotland. But that is no compensation to the people of southern Britain who have lost a beautiful and useful tree.

Elm has been used for a variety of purposes, perhaps the most important being coffin making. It is seldom used for furniture because it seems to warp and twist unless very carefully kiln-dried. So its main use was for coffins and packing cases since it may be nailed without splitting, due to its dense non-fissile nature. Because of these properties and its resistance to waterlogging elm has been used for bridge piles, wheel hubs and boatbuilding – and even street paving-blocks were once made from it. Elm is no less useful to the natural world and provides a nesting site for rooks, crows, owls and many other bird species. To deter grazing by stock it has, like its cousin the nettle, hairy leaves but, unlike the nettle, no sting. One particular part of the tree has been used as a food by Man. The cambium layer (just under the bark) contains a rich supply of proteins and carbohydrates in spring. This nutritious food was once collected and sold under the name of slippery elm. It was an easily digested food for invalids and patients suffering from gastric disorders.

Oak

Although oaks often form large areas of woodland they are at their best when they stand alone, either towering majestically above a hedgerow or in the middle of a field. Our two native oaks are *Quercus robur* (pedunculate oak or common oak), common in the south on heavier soils, and *Quercus petraea* (sessile oak), more frequently found in the north and west on lighter soils. Acorns and flowers of *Q. petraea* do not have stalks whereas those of *Q. robur* are carried on long stalks. The underside of sessile oak leaves is often hairy. However, identification is frequently complicated by hybridisation between the two. Oaks are important as harbourers of the greatest variety and number of insect species. When they occur in a hedgerow it is often possible to find oak-apples, the pupal chamber of *Biorhiza pallida*, a type of wasp. Generations alternate their habitats and eggs of the next generation are laid at ground level on the roots of oaks. Many other interesting galls are to be found on oak leaves.

Because of the practice of mechanised hedge

Left Marble galls on oak are caused by gall wasps.

Right Spangle galls on an oak leaf.

trimming it is unlikely that oaks will survive in the future as hedgerow trees. In meadows and parkland, large specimens may linger on for hundreds of years but, unless replanting schemes are instigated, the oak is going to be an increasingly rare sight. Another possible reason for the oak's decline in popularity is Man's impatience. What modern man would plant a tree that he would never see reach maturity? It takes two hundred years or more before oak trees begin to attain the massive proportions we associate with them. There is a body of opinion which holds that even today's prized specimens – massive, majestic oaks of mighty girth – are poor-quality survivors of a far superior race, all the finest trees having been used as timber and only inferior specimens remain. That is a matter of opinion but, if oaks are felled at maturity, their girth may be up to 12m and their height 40m, and they produce many thousands of pounds worth of timber. But what a loss to

nature and the many dependent species!

Oaks are felled for timber at the age of about two hundred years before their wood has become riddled by insects or discoloured by fungi. Principal uses were for shipbuilding, furniture and boatbuilding. Hedgerow oaks provided a good supply of the crooked limbs that could be used in the framework of boats. One unusual feature of oak which cannot be reproduced faithfully by the forger's surface staining is the way in which it blackens with age. Jacobean oak furniture is almost black in colour, whereas later furniture has not attained such depth of pigmentation.

Ash

Ash (*Fraxinus excelsior*) is often found in the same environments as oak and, like oak, is one of the last trees in leaf. An old country rhyme of very little truth is 'If oak before ash we're in for a splash. If ash before oak we're in for a soak'. It is more likely that the trees are

Oak cherry gall

governed by past weather than by future conditions. However, the last tree to shelter under in a gale is a large ash. It is remarkable how the meandering, almost horizontal, branches seem to outgrow their strength. In high winds, when their leaves are made heavier by rain, or when branches are weighed down by snow, ash trees have an alarming tendency to shed a branch with a sudden crack like the sound of a whip. These cast-off branches, often further weakened by rot and insects, provide farmers with a valuable source of winter fuel. Many ashes exist for years in a sort of semi-moribund condition, occasionally shedding a branch or two, before eventually succumbing.

Ash was once a common hedge tree, but has several disadvantages now that its timber is no longer needed to make agricultural implements and tool handles, and even spear shafts. One reason for its lack of popularity is that ash takes a lot of nourishment from the soil, inhibiting surrounding growth. Also, the drip from ash leaves poisons surrounding foliage.

Beech

Beech (*Fagus sylvatica*) has a preference for the rich chalk soils found in southern areas. Despite this, beech has been used as a hedge tree, where, if clipped regularly, it attains a dense growth of foliage borne on a twisting, interwoven network of branches. Although leaves turn brown and are shed in autumn, recently trimmed hedgerows retain their leaves, due to chemical changes, throughout the winter. Thus they provide good stock shelter from wind, rain and snow. For this reason, even though beeches set seed more regularly in the south, they are used in hedges even in southern Scotland. The wood of mature beech trees has been used extensively in chair manufacture and turning, but tends to warp if used for high-quality cabinet work. Since beech drip has similar effects to ash drip on surrounding vegetation, the tree has

Above Ash keys in autumn.

Right Ash flowers in spring.

declined in popularity as a hedging or shelter-belt tree.

The rose family

The largest and most useful range of hedging plants belong to the rose family (Rosaceae). Many members of this varied family provide animals and humans with lasting supplies of winter food. By far the most abundantly used hedging plant is hawthorn. There are two distinct varieties. *Crataegus monogyna*, or common hawthorn, rarely exceeds a height of 10m but is tough, thorny and resilient enough to withstand high winds, salt spray and cold weather. Midland hawthorn (*C. oxyacanthoides*) is less hardy. The leaves of both are a favourite food for cattle and sheep, which are able to browse on new growth until the thorns harden. As a result, many hawthorns of open fields are mere stunted humps, unable to reach anything near their full height. Only when a leader grows above animal height are such exposed trees able to produce a good head. Hawthorn leaves are quite palatable to humans and were always supposed by country people to taste of bread and cheese, though it takes some imagination to believe this. However, the berries make a drinkable wine, albeit with a rather astringent taste. Perhaps the best aspect of haw wine is its colour, which reminds one of a good rosé. But take care, the berries have been used as a drug. Some of the acids they contain were extracted and used to treat patients suffering from hypertension, cardiac disorders and insomnia. I imagine the remedy for the latter would be to drink a bottle of haw wine and then retire to bed! Since hawthorn berries are a favourite food for thrushes, perhaps they are best left on the bush.

Hawthorn plays a key role in mythology and legend and maypole dancers still dance through hoops of may blossom (or whitethorn) in ancient fertility celebrations throughout the country on the first of May. That is, if the blossom is out. This was less of a problem before the introduction of the Gregorian calendar in 1762, since previously the first of May fell fourteen days earlier than it does nowadays. In northern areas flowering may be retarded by a month or more, but it is well worth waiting for the avalanches of creamy white fragrant blossom in a good year. There is an old term relating to weather lore. Cold periods occurring at the time when the hawthorn was in flower were known as 'whitethorn winters', though it may be that the term described the wintry appearance of the countryside in a good blossom year. A similar term was 'blackthorn winter', which perhaps referred to the frequent cold snaps that occur when the sloes, or blackthorns, flower in late March or April.

Blackthorn is a relative of hawthorn but flowers earlier, before it produces foliage. Blackthorn is a common hedgerow tree of chalk and limestone areas, where it seems to thrive better and produce more fruit than on acid or clay soils. But a blackthorn winter may shrivel the flowers in bud or deter bees from pollinating the flowers, and the end result is a poor crop of those lustrous blue-black fruits which make such good wine or sloe gin. Yet the fruit that makes such a warming wine is bitter and acid to the taste and no amount of sugar proves otherwise. The blackthorn has been improved by selective breeding to produce the damson of horticulture, a fruit which does well in favoured localities such as the Vale of Evesham and the Lyth Valley near Kendal.

Blackthorn's self-explanatory Latin name is *Prunus spinosa* and its long spines are a strong deterrent to browsing or straying stock. But growth may be very straggly and uneven, so hawthorn is preferred for hedging. Blackthorn has several close relatives, including cherry plum and wild plum or bullace. Many variations occur in the wild and some of these may be the result of chance crossing with garden plums or damsons, or even the result of a discarded plum stone.

Other close relatives are our three wild cherries. The gean (*Prunus avium*) is the most abundant and largest of the three, being widely distributed in fields and hedges throughout the country. Its bronze-tinted, toothed oval leaves give a display of spring colour which is equalled only by the froth of white blossom which opens shortly afterwards. The heart-shaped black or red berries are acidic and consist largely of stone. Birds, however, love them and the gean is soon denuded of its fruit in autumn, though humans prefer the improved varieties of cherry produced from the gean by selective breeding. A distinctive feature of all cherries, wild or cultivated, is their smooth red-brown bark which covers a close-grained warm-coloured wood. The wood is much prized by carvers, as are other fruit woods, for its untemperamental working qualities. Another cherry, *Prunus cerasus*, has similar characteristics but may never attain the same height or elegance as the gean. It, too, has been taken into cultivation and morello cherries are said to be derivatives.

The least edible of our three wild hedgerow cherries produces a small, black, bitter fruit. Its Latin name is *Prunus padus* and it is known to countrymen as bird cherry. It is a tree of northern regions, not naturalised south of a line from Leicester to the Bristol Channel. Unlike other cherries, the creamy-white ragged flowers of bird cherry are carried in long, drooping spikes. They are scented – some say rather like hawthorn, but to my nose the perfume smells more like carrion. Bird cherry is a common species in ancient hedgerows and around old woodland clearings. In northern scrub woodland pastures it is often the most abundant species.

Crab apples really have little need to protect their fruits by spines, but some of the true wild crabs (*Malus sylvestris*) are armed with blunted spines. The lack of spines is said to denote *Malus domestica*, a degenerate cultivated apple, but it is very difficult to decide whether a particular tree is a degenerate cultivated apple or a true wild variety so I tend to classify them all as crabs. Long ago, before human tastes were conditioned to sugar with everything, crabs were eaten as a fruit. Shakespeare refers to them being roasted. Other writers have told of hedgehogs being partial to the fruit and collecting crabs by rolling amongst them, then carrying a load away impaled on their spines, though such stories may, as we shall see later, have a less colourful explanation. Foxes, too, are said to relish crabs. Certainly, cattle and sheep appear to enjoy the less acidic types and slugs readily devour any that are left lying on the ground. Birds are very partial to them and will spoil a whole crop by pecking a hole in each apple. Insect larvae do not seem to attack crab apples as keenly as they would devour domestic types. Perhaps high acidity is a deterrent.

Crabs do not provide dense hedging material and are never planted in hedges nowadays, so those that remain are usually bird-sown or survivors of old woodland edges. Their fruits can be used to make crab apple jelly and also a light effervescent wine, but plenty of sugar is needed to nullify their acidity. Apple wood has a dense-grained quality and like cherry is excellent for carving or turning. One of its major uses was in domestic implements and utensils. This may provide a reason for the widespread occurrence of crabs in hedgerows.

Roses and brambles are almost considered to be weeds by most farmers, yet they are good gap fillers and hedge binders even if their thorns are a nuisance. To the naturalist and countryman they represent a valuable source of food for man and animals. *Rosa canina*, the dog rose, with its pink flowers in June, is our most widespread wild hedgerow rose, far more common than the white-flowered trailing rose and the long-styled rose, which both wind and trail through other hedge shrubs. Rose hips are rich in vitamin C and were collected in large amounts during the last war when citrus fruits were in short supply. The Ministry of Health supervised a collection

Dog roses

Left Haws – a winter feast for thrushes.

Opposite (top) Crab apple blossom

Opposite (bottom) Crab apples look good to eat, but contain a large amount of unpalatable malic acid.

Below Bird cherry blossom in spring.

scheme and thousands of tons of hips were collected by schoolchildren, throughout the war, to be processed into rose hip syrup. It is worth remembering, although few people either buy or take the trouble to make the syrup nowadays, that rose hips contain four times as much vitamin C as blackcurrants. The secret of making use of all the hips' vitamin content it to use them freshly picked. They should be pulped and saturated with boiling water to destroy an enzyme which decomposes the vitamin. The solution is then sieved, sweetened and bottled. Prolonged boiling of the hips also destroys the vitamin C. The vitamin is used to combat scurvy and gives some resistance to the common cold, too.

A less altruistic use of rose hips I remember from childhood is as 'itchy backs'. We used to use the hairy seeds as a substitute for itching powder and put them down some unfortunate person's back. Apparently the seeds do not have an irritant action on the birds and mammals by which they are sown. Rose seeds will not grow unless they have been subjected to the rigours of a British winter. Gardeners

stratify them by making up a box of hips, sandwiched between layers of sand, which is left out all winter. Dog roses are sometimes used as stock for grafting purposes.

Compared with their relative the bramble, the flavour of rose hips is rather insipid and this is probably the reason why most people prefer blackberries for making pies, though rose hips were once used in the confectionery trade. To make a palatable pie filling, each hip had to be cleaned and all the irritant seeds and hairs scraped out.

An interesting aspect of roses is their ability to react to the action of a gall-forming wasp, *Diplolepis rosae*. Female wasps lay their eggs in unopened buds, which react strangely (in a way which is as yet not satisfactorily explained) by forming a multi-chambered structure surrounded by red mossy filaments – the robin's pincushion. Each chamber produces an adult insect the following spring, even though by this time the old gall looks dead, black and decayed. An interesting experiment is to take a gall home, keep it cool over the winter, then place it on a bed of sand covered by a jam jar on an inside window ledge where, with patience, you will see the occupants emerge.

Brambles make superb hedge repairers in the event of another shrub's demise but, once established, are difficult to control. Yet they provide us with the most widely appreciated fruit of autumn, the blackberry. Researchers have identified more than 2,000 micro-species of *Rubus fruticosus* and a walk along any hedgerow at picking time emphasises that blackberry is a very variable species. Some berries tend to be large and juicy with few seeds, others are nearly all seed, and some carry only a few fleshy segments. Others seem to have crossed with a near relative – the dewberry – and their berries have a bluish sloe-like bloom. The leaves and thorns also vary considerably.

Notice the similarity between the methods by which strawberries and brambles produce new shoots. Just as a strawberry plant puts out rooting runners, a bramble grows down-curving stems which root and throw up new growth wherever they touch the ground. Eventually an original seedling may be surrounded by hundreds of its own clones.

Trees of the *Sorbus* genus form yet another part of the Rosaceae tribe. Mountain ash or rowan is seldom used as a hedging shrub but often appears in hedgerows, where it provides an early source of berries for newly arrived fieldfares and redwings each autumn. Rowan (*Sorbus aucuparia*) seems to become more abundant as one travels northwards. There is an historical reason for this. Once the tree was regarded as a good luck symbol with properties to ward off evil spirits and many Scottish crofts were surrounded by a hedge of rowans as protection against evil. Rowan berries make a second-rate substitute for cranberries and can be used as a sweet sauce for game – but they require a lot of sugar to disguise their latent bitterness, though their red-orange colour looks appetising enough.

Sorbus aria, or whitebeam, carries bunches of orange-red berries which taste even more bitter than rowan berries. However, birds are not deterred by their bitterness and starlings often descend upon a whitebeam and strip it of all its berries in a few hours. 'Beam' is the old Saxon word for tree (*baum* in German). The use of the word meaning 'roof supports' derives from the fact that whole trees were needed to make house beams. *Sorbus aria* gained the name whitebeam because the undersides of its leaves are covered in white down. Several other closely allied species of *Sorbus* occur in various parts of Britain.

Holly

No chapter on hedgerow trees would be complete without the holly (*Ilex aquifolium*), one of our toughest native trees with its spiny dark-green leaves and smooth grey bark. Holly makes a useful hedging plant and grows densely if regularly trimmed. In the past it was used as a fodder plant, providing much-needed nourishment for starving cattle during the long winter months, since cattle will eat holly despite its spines if they are hungry enough. It is said that the spines developed as a protection against browsing cattle and this theory may be confirmed by the fact that some hollies grow leaves with fewer spines as they attain a greater height. Some subspecies do not bear spines at all. There are even some cultivated varieties, developed from natural sports, with golden berries or with variegated leaves. Some trees, indeed, never bear fruits (termed drupes – like plums and cherries) because they bear only male flowers. Other hollies bear female flowers and produce berries by cross-fertilisation with a male tree, whilst some hollies bear flowers with both stamens and stigmas.

Holly is a useful wood with a dense white texture. It turns and carves readily and has been used to make chessmen. Holly branches make good walking sticks and many a prospective stick is watched over jealously until it reaches the correct size. Readers of Surtees may remember the foolish Mr Jogglebury Crowder (in *Mr Sponge's Sporting Tour*) who spent all his time searching for suitable sticks, which he took from hedgerows and copses, to carve into likenesses of famous people, believing that he was making a valuable legacy for his children. Holly grows so slowly that it is a pity to chop down a tree unless it is diseased or needed for a definite purpose – certainly not for firewood, although the wood burns readily with fierce brilliance even when freshly felled. One of my favourite activities, though a sad one, is to burn holly trimmings after Christmas to see how they crackle and twist in the fire and sparkle with bursts of flame. Perhaps our ancestors derived a similar pleasure when they burnt yule logs from fir trees.

Elder

Elders (*Sambucus nigra*) were frequent escapes from the cottage gardens of centuries ago, where they were often grown as a fruit and for their medicinal qualities. Now the trees are rarely grown in gardens but thrive in hedgerows, particularly where disturbed soil of high nitrogenous content gives their seeds a chance to germinate and surmount surrounding vegetation. Elders flower and fruit best near heavily manured stock pens, but a good substitute site is a hedgerow bank where badgers have excavated their residences and deposited faeces. Because elder grows quickly its branches are very pithy. With the pith removed they have been used as musical instruments and as blowpipes by little boys and have even been fashioned into simple water pipes.

Although the wood from older trees is useful as an inferior type of fruitwood, the main product of elder is its crop of glossy purple-black berries, borne in large umbels in autumn. In the past country people have used the berries in pies and jams, but their most frequent use was in wine. Our British elderberries were of such a high quality that, it is recorded, they were exported to Bordeaux in the Middle Ages to augment the grapes of that region because in those days Bordeaux grapes lacked the astringent qualities of tannic acid necessary to produce a good claret. Elderberries in small quantities made up the deficit. Nowadays, home-made wine makers often use the berries without the addition of grapes and a well matured elder wine resembles port in colour and flavour. The berries have other uses, too. They contain small quantities of organic acids, oils and vitamin C. Used as a cordial or an infusion, they reduce inflammation of the respiratory system and reduce fever in cases of colds and influenza. In fact, a good remedy for a cold is to take half a cup of warmed elderberry wine, dissolve in it a quarter of a teaspoon of cinammon, and drink the soothing and spicy mixture, piping hot, just before you go to bed.

Above Rowan berries may be used as a substitute for cranberries in preserves.

Opposite (top) Burnet rose may be found on calcareous heaths.

Opposite (bottom) Rose hips are a rich source of vitamin C.

Currants

Few country lanes are without their quota of the *Ribes* genus. In early spring, when blackthorn is in blossom but before hawthorn is in leaf, the only greenery in a thorn hedge may be provided by an occasional gooseberry bush. There may be two reasons for the shrub's appearance in hedgerows. It may be the result of bird-sown seed or, since gooseberry leaves and twigs look very like hawthorn, bushes may have been planted in mistake for hawthorn. Gooseberries (*Ribes uva-crispa*) display much variation in appearance. Some are almost spineless whilst others are as spiny as hedgehogs. Some fruits are large and not very acidic; others small, hairy and sour. Gooseberries from some bushes, when ripe, take on a reddish hue, almost appearing to be crossed with blackcurrant. With the correct amount of sugar they all make good pies and jams and are far less insipid in taste than many garden varieties. Gooseberry bushes are good hedging material until denuded of foliage by gooseberry sawfly larvae (*Nematus ribesii*). The fruits are not attacked by these voracious leaf eaters, which have three or four broods a year and pupate in the ground at the base of their host.

Blackcurrants (*Ribes nigrum*) are also occasionally found in hedgerows, where their lack of thorns limits their usefulness as a hedging shrub. Few pickers are fortunate enough to find a really good crop of wild blackcurrants, since the berries are produced in small amounts on wild varieties and those that ripen are soon eaten by birds (so, too, are the fruits of the redcurrant, which occurs in similar locations). Blackcurrant may be attacked by gooseberry sawflies and is also prone to attacks of big bud – an irritation caused by the big bud mite – which produces distended, rounded (rather than elongated) buds in early spring. Another feature of the mite is that it may act as a carrier of virus disease, which debilitates most wild blackcurrants, causing restricted growth and reduced yields of fruit.

When currant-like shrubs are not in fruit it is very difficult to distinguish between black- and redcurrants. The difference is that the leaves of blackcurrants have an aroma (not unlike cats), whereas those of redcurrants are odourless.

In more northerly limestone regions of Britain, mountain currant (*Ribes alpinum*) replaces the other currant species. Its fruits are greenish-red and rather tasteless but much loved by birds.

A curious instance of cross-breeding in the wild is the occurrence of a hybrid between gooseberry and blackcurrant. In all aspects but one the hybrid resembles a halfway stage between both parents. The fruits are midway in size, colour and flavour between those of gooseberry and currant, but for some strange reason the bushes are much more spiny than any type of gooseberry and almost resemble cactus in their prickliness. Horticultural varieties are known as Worcester berries.

As we have seen, hedgerows have many fascinating historical and biological aspects, exist in most parts of the country and are easily studied. What is more, the techniques of hedge dating can add interest to a country walk as this occupation involves careful cataloguing of species, so recognition and note taking are improved at the same time. It is also rewarding to adopt a particular length of hedgerow and over the years record the type and numbers of species of plants and animals to be found along its length. The catalogue may produce an astonishing variety of species. But perhaps the most satisfying hedgerow occupation is to gather a good collection of recipes – then to go out, collect and use the produce of the hedgerows.

6 MAMMALS

Wild cattle

Primitive breeds of domesticated animals may be seen in many farm museums throughout Britain, where their continued existence is assured thanks to the painstaking efforts of devotees and members of breed preservation societies. It is well worth preserving ancient breeds of domesticated stock purely from a sentimental or conservation-conscious attitude. But by far the most important reason for conserving any species, whether domesticated or wild, is to ensure continuation of a set of unique genes which may be needed by future generations. Many of our oldest breeds of cattle and sheep have developed particular immunities and characteristics which are not found in modern varieties. Unfortunately, Britain's surviving wild cattle, sheep and goats are not truly wild and must be classified as feral, though in the case of the wild white cattle the position is arguable.

Wild white cattle still exist in one of Britain's oldest enclosed parklands. At Chillingham in Northumberland they have lived undisturbed since they were driven into the 1,100-acre park when it was enclosed in the thirteenth century. Before that time, it is said, white cattle roamed freely and were hunted in surrounding forests. Were these cattle, even in those times, feral descendants of ancient domestic cattle or were they truly wild? Whichever is the true explanation, the *Bos taurus* of Chillingham exhibits many characteristics of a truly wild breed. Like deer, the cows hide their newborn calves in dense patches of bracken or rank undergrowth for several days, returning only to suckle them. Also, white cattle distrust human interference

and only recently have they taken to eating the hay provided in severe winters. Previously such help was shunned, presumably because the cattle detected Man's scent on the hay. At mating time battles take place to decide which bull will become master of the herd and pass on his genes to the next generation. As well as showing hostility towards his fellows, a master bull is liable to charge humans if they walk between him and his herd.

The number of cattle in the Chillingham herd has suffered major fluctuations from time to time as a result of severe winters and lack of food. But the natural vigour of the herd has always won through despite the fact that these cattle have been inbred for centuries. So far as is known no outsiders have been introduced since the time of enclosure. Geneticists might argue that inbreeding enfeebles vigour and fertility. Chillingham cattle lack neither. In fact, recent genetic research with other animals has disproved many of the old theories and suggests that incest may be useful in eradicating undesirable characteristics. For, after a stage where weaklings are born (these, of course, die in nature), all harmful genes have cancelled themselves out, leaving only desirable genes and a race with added vigour, hardiness and resistance to disease. This may have been the case at Chillingham.

Although there are other white cattle in Britain, none are of pure breed and some have had to be crossed with other cattle to maintain the type. The Chillingham cattle are unique in two aspects: they have red ears and their horns are more upright than those of other white cattle.

Sheep and goats

Sheep and goats belong to the same family as cattle, the Bovidae. No native wild breeds of goat remain but several feral herds exist in remote areas, where they may originally have escaped from domestication. On the other hand, goats have been introduced to precipitous crags by farmers in order to graze

Wild white cattle at Chillingham.

inaccessible ledges and deter less agile sheep from venturing into danger. Several feral herds of goats exist in Scotland, Wales and Ireland, living in small herds ever alert for the presence of man. At the first hint of danger they clamber over cliffs where even a good

rock climber would think twice before risking his life.

Our most primitive breed of sheep, the Soay, resembles a goat in its long-legged agility. I have often followed sheep tracks in mountainous areas because domesticated sheep tend to follow reasonably safe routes. Not so the Soay sheep. On the island of Hirta, part of the St Kilda group, their trails are like goat tracks, meandering over precipitous ledges over a thousand feet above foaming Atlantic rollers. These sure-footed creatures are the remnants of flocks left on Soay when the human inhabitants of nearby Hirta were evacuated to the Scottish mainland in 1930. Originally they came from Viking stock. They live on and thrive where Man failed to eke out an existence, on the main island of Hirta, to which they were removed in 1932.

Soay sheep are also to be found in more accessible places: several wildlife parks and specialist breeders have perpetuated the breed on mainland Britain. They differ from domesticated sheep in several respects. Their

Scay sheep on St Kilda.

appearance is much more goatlike and their wool needs no clipping – plucking suffices. In the wild the old coat gradually falls out and breeders have found that gradual plucking is better than a once-and-for-all trim which may leave the sheep prone to respiratory infections. Their horns differ from those of domestic sheep, being thicker, stouter and more like those of goats.

Lagomorphs

Even the rabbit (*Oryctolagus cuniculus*) is not a truly indigenous species, having been introduced from Europe by the Normans shortly after the conquest. Their use as food dates back even further in Europe and there are records that rabbit flesh was a favourite delicacy amongst the Romans, who kept the animals in specially constructed walled enclosures known as *leporaria*. In Britain, warrens, under the charge of a warrener, were constructed on many of the great estates.

Above Rabbit infected with myxomatosis

Right Rabbits were introduced by the Normans.

These enclosures were made of stone and, where possible, were built down to bedrock to avoid escape by tunnelling. Even so, some rabbits escaped into the wild and bred so prolifically that they soon became a menace to agriculture until by the early 1950s the British population was estimated to be as many as 100 million. This had been achieved despite the fact that foxes, stoats, weasels, buzzards, poachers, legitimate trappers and many other animal predators were doing their bit to keep numbers down.

Up to 1953 rabbit was a regular item in most people's diet. (Before the Second World War rabbits were usually sold at a shilling apiece.) All this changed with the introduction of the *Myxomatosis cuniculus* virus. Earlier attempts to introduce the disease by releasing infected laboratory animals had failed when the diseased animals died without infecting other members of the experimental colony on the island of Skokholm. Eventually it was realised that the carrier of the virus, the rabbit flea, was absent from Skokholm. When diseased animals were released on mainland Britain the rabbit population was all but wiped out by the rapid spread of a virulent disease to which rabbits had no natural resistance. I remember the early years of myxomatosis when every country walk became a long catalogue of dead and dying rabbits. Everywhere there was the stink of death and decay. Only when the damage had been done did the Ministry of Agriculture admit what a dreadful scourge had been released. Fortunately the disease was specific to rabbits and no other species were affected. Experiments had been carried out to determine this before the disease was introduced into the wild. Short-term gains were almost instantaneous; farmers were able to graze more sheep and cattle on land where, previously, rabbits had grazed. However, due to public repugnance at the sight of rabbits dying miserably with pus-swollen eyes, game dealers were never again able to sell rabbits in the high numbers in which they had been sold earlier in the century.

As happens with every outbreak of disease, some animals were infected but managed to survive. These became the progenitors of a new myxomatosis-resistant strain of rabbit, which by the early 1960s was building up the population again. Nowadays many rabbits are still infected by the disease but decreasing numbers are killed by it, though many fall a prey to other predators whilst incapacitated. In some areas population levels appear to be approaching their old levels and the very prosperity of farming may once again be threatened. Allowing for inflation, if rabbits were to attain pre-1950 population levels financial loss due to rabbit damage could be in the region of £500 million per year through-

out Britain at a conservative estimate. It seems that rabbits are here to stay and there is little man can do about it. Perhaps once again we should turn disaster to advantage and renew the fight with our knives and forks. This would also help our balance of payments, since the majority of rabbits eaten in Britain are bred in China from domesticated British stock exported some years ago.

British rabbits really do breed in the proverbial manner and a doe may produce five litters in a breeding season, which lasts from February to September. Does from early litters are capable of producing their own offspring by the autumn of the year of their birth since they may become pregnant at four months old and gestation lasts a mere thirty days. At birth rabbits are virtually naked, but they soon develop a thick coat of fur. Eleven days after birth their eyes open and in three weeks rabbits are sufficiently well developed to venture above ground and begin feeding on grass and other herbage. When young rabbits cease to depend upon their mother they are very often forced to move to the outer edges of the colony, particularly if they are the offspring of parents who are low in the hierarchy of dominance or if population levels are high. Perhaps there is some advantage in living away from the centre of a large colony, since food may be more easily found. On the other hand, outlying burrows are often the first to be visited by predators.

Rabbits eat similar types of herbage to that favoured by sheep. If superior food is available – cabbage, lettuce, turnip, carrots – they will be sure to take advantage of it, so their presence is definitely not welcomed by arable farmers. In winter, when snow lies thick on the ground, rabbits rarely venture out because not only are their movements hampered – and they are more likely to be caught by predators – but also they dislike having wet fur. They are aided in their idleness and unwillingness to come out in inclement weather by their ability to redigest their own faecal pellets. These soft,

Hares have longer hind legs than rabbits.

mucus-covered faeces are swallowed without chewing and are redigested to extract any remaining nourishment which may have been missed (or added as a result of bacteriological action) the first time through. Obviously there is a limit to this process and the results of refection are hard, dry fibrous pellets, which are not eaten a third time. Hares also practise refection in periods of food shortage.

The other common lagomorph found in fields is the brown hare (*Lepus capensis*), easily distinguishable from the rabbit by its larger size, longer hind legs, more reddish-brown coat and longer black-tipped ears. Unlike rabbits, hares do not live below ground and do not, therefore, run off to hide at the first sign of human intrusion. They stand their ground, staying perfectly still with flattened ears by a tuft of grass in a form (grassy hollow) until, at the last moment, often just as one is about to step on them, they leap into

motion and 'hare away' over the fields. Hares frequent pastures and arable land and could be just as destructive as rabbits if their numbers were greater, as they were in the nineteenth century. However, in 1880, the Ground Game Act was passed. This changed the status of hares from sporting animals to pests and farmers were allowed to shoot them whenever crops were threatened. Since then hares have been less numerous, though they experienced a revival when myxomatosis was first introduced and, as a consequence, more food became available to them.

Hares appear to be most numerous in spring, when, utterly oblivious of onlookers, they dance, leap and box in mad courtship routines. Six weeks after mating up to five leverets are produced. These perfect miniature replicas of their parents have fur and all their faculties at birth and are soon able to move about, though for a while they are left in concealment among rank vegetation. Female hares may have up to four litters in a season

A young leveret

and may give birth in any month of the year, though spring is the time when most leverets are born. Like rabbits, they are able to re-absorb embryos in times of food shortage.

Hares and rabbits suffer predation by a similar range of predators, though rabbits seem to be more vulnerable because of their underground lifestyle and comparative lack of speed when above ground. It is often said that rabbits are terrified to the point of petri-fication by stoats and weasels. I was fortunate enough to witness one exception to the rule.

A stoat was out rabbiting, delving into every likely hole along a bank of old, gnarled hawthorns, looking for rodents, nestlings or, better still, rabbits. Suddenly the stoat's manner became more urgent as he seemed to catch the scent of something at the base of an oak whose twisted roots had been exposed by soil erosion, leaving a multitude of holes and hiding places beneath. In an instant he disappeared to ground, giving me one last glimpse of a black-tipped tail.

I waited for what seemed ages, but in reality must have been only a few seconds. Then, out of one of the larger holes bounded a large doe rabbit, closely followed by a youngster not much more than three weeks old, followed by another, and another, until six or eight young rabbits had popped out of the hole as quickly as if an invisible conjurer was producing them by magic. Hard on the heels of the last rabbit – the most diminutive of them all – came the stoat.

With a bound he seized his victim by the back of the neck. The result was a treble shriek, so heart-rending that the doe, whose only idea had been to put as great a distance as possible between herself and the stoat, must have suffered some pangs of maternal instinct. She stopped. She turned and ran back towards the scene of the crime, past her other fleeing offspring, oblivious of any danger to herself. The stoat was too preoccupied with his prospective meal to notice this change of attitude in the old doe. As she leapt into the fray she reared on her hind legs and, with fore legs raised like a march hare, proceeded to give the stoat a boxing lesson.

This was too much for the startled stoat, who yielded under a rain of blows and turned to flee, utterly confused that the laws of nature had been reversed. The doe pursued him for twenty yards to the bank of a stream. Only when the stoat jumped into the water and swam to the far bank to save himself did the doe abandon the chase.

But one exception does not disprove the rule. This is the only case I have seen when the tables were turned on the aggressor. On several other occasions I have witnessed stoats

Stoat, first on the gamekeeper's gibbet.

catching rabbits too terrified to defend themselves. In one incident a stoat pursued a rabbit round and round in circles and figures of eight, slowly gaining on and drawing nearer to his prey. After about a minute the rabbit either tired or gave up and stopped abruptly. The stoat dispatched the rabbit by going for the back of the neck. After a piercing shriek of agony the rabbit died. There were several unanswered questions in my mind after seeing this attack. Why did the rabbit fail to seek shelter underground? Why did it give in to the stoat? Most interestingly, the chase took place on the edge of a grouse moor and was watched by several grouse and rabbits who took no evasive action, even though the pursued and pursuer ran amongst them. Seemingly, a stoat has a one-track mind and pursues the original scent unerringly.

Mustelids

Stoats are said to be myopic, which could explain why the static observers were not threatened. They also have a curious habit of standing upright on their hind legs and staring around. Like several other members of the Mustelidae family, stoats are very playful. This is almost a common feature of predators and play is said to be practice for hunting. I have seen a stoat play with a freshly killed vole, just like a cat plays with a mouse, juggling with it then putting it down and making practice jumps and pounces. This playfulness is sometimes turned to a stoat's advantage, whether consciously or otherwise, when stoats use the fox's technique of 'charming' or playfully rolling about on the ground to attract an audience close enough for a quick pounce.

Stoats have long been thought of as vermin – justifiably in some cases – and many a keeper's gibbet has its quota of victims. However, their useful role in controlling rabbits is often underplayed and their predation on game overstated. Years ago stoats were hunted for another reason. In winter the

Weasel on the alert for food.

coat of some stoats turns white, except for the black tip of their tail, providing the ermine (the stoat's Latin name is *Mustela erminae*) so prized by royalty. Portraits of Queen Elizabeth I depict her in ermine robes. But not all stoats turn white in winter. The northern areas of Britain, which are colder, seem to contain a greater proportion of white stoats. Also, more females undergo the colour change, which may not be caused by the coldness of the present winter but rather by conditions during the preceding winter. Length of day also plays a part in controlling colour change.

Stoats usually live solitarily in separate territories. Mating occurs in the summer, but embryos are not usually implanted until March of the next year. An average of six youngsters are born in a nest situated in a hole in a tree or bank. They are suckled for up to six weeks and are able to kill for themselves at about ten weeks old. Females are much smaller than males and this is also true of weasels. The breeding of weasels is similar in most aspects to that of stoats, but there is no delayed implantation in weasels.

Weasels are absent from Ireland but the Irish make up for the deficit by calling stoats 'weasels'. However, in mainland Britain, weasels inhabit much the same territory as stoats, frequenting dry stone walls and hedge banks. There is little overlap in prey species and weasels tend to specialise in small rodents, though they sometimes kill chickens or game chicks. Nevertheless, they do far more good than harm, yet are still persecuted by keepers to the same extent as stoats and are often seen suspended from a fence as a discouragement to others.

Our other farmland representative of the Mustelidae is the much maligned and cruelly persecuted badger (*Meles meles*). Badgers love to inhabit old hedgerow banks, where they excavate whole networks of intricate tunnels and chambers with several entrances and means of escape. Their strong, long-clawed fore limbs are ideally adapted to digging through heavy soils and even their ears are adapted to a burrowing, underground life. To keep out dust when burrowing a badger's ears are closed by muscular action. The very fact that badgers defend themselves vigorously has jeopardised their existence. They were once dug out of their sets to provide sport for dogs and, apparently, people used to revel in the gory sight of a badger literally locking his jaw on the throat of some poor cur. For more information on the old sport of badger baiting, read the poem 'The Badger' by John Clare. What the poet does not mention is the fact that badgers were often nailed down by the tail to prevent them from chasing the terriers.

In 1878 badger baiting was made illegal, but even today there are still people with a perverted idea of fun who continue the practice to provide sport for their working terriers. There can be no excuse for such callous behaviour and the only way to stop such malevolent acts taking place is to impose heavy fines when diggers are caught.

Recently the Ministry of Agriculture, in a report prepared by Lord Zuckerman, blamed badgers for transmitting bovine tuberculosis via their faeces. With overprecipitate zeal, many badger colonies in south-west England were exterminated by gassing. The report had confused human T.B. with bovine T.B. In fact there are very few recorded cases of bovine T.B. in humans. What the Zuckerman report omitted to mention was that, prior to 1960, 30 per cent of Britain's dairy herds were infected with bovine T.B. If so many cattle were infected, then a high percentage of badgers must also have been infected (if we accept the report's conclusions that badgers are the carriers). When the disease was almost eradicated after the early 1960s, why weren't herds reinfected by badgers still carrying bovine T.B.? In short, if badgers didn't infect cattle then, why were they able to infect them in the early 1980s? Due to pressure from various sources the gassing plan was abandoned — too late for those badgers who had already suffered. However, Ministry scientists appear to be unconvinced by the weight of scientific opinion which has been directed against their extermination plan. At the time of writing I have information that Ministry scientists are planning to take badgers from Sussex in an attempt to prove a link between badgers and bovine T.B. This prospective action is, in itself, a virtual admission that they hadn't proved anything the first time round. Surely the most logical hypothesis to work on would be to assume that cattle are themselves carriers of bovine T.B.

Badgers are clean and tidy animals in their bodily habits and regularly change their bedding of bracken and dry grasses. Droppings are deposited in latrines. They are rarely seen in daytime and, perhaps because of centuries of persecution, usually come out when it is dark, although they sometimes appear at dusk in summer months. Their nocturnal hunting for a wide variety of food is effected mainly by scenting and grubbing about with nose close to the ground. Small mammals, young rabbits, grubs, worms, roots and fruit are all acceptable and badgers will even tear apart wasps' nests in order to extract grubs. By dawn they have usually returned to their earth, where the day is spent in sleep or idleness. The only signs remaining above ground are freshly disturbed earth and broad five-toed footprints.

In common with stoats, badgers regulate their breeding times by delayed implantation. Mating may take place at any time, but the main period is in early spring. Fertilised eggs do not implant in the uterus until the following December, about nine months later. After a gestation of eight weeks, young badgers are born in February. They remain in the warmth of the set during the cold days of spring, but are weaned and ready to forage just when large amounts of food become available.

Hibernation

One of the false assumptions made about badgers by past generations of naturalists was that they hibernated. This is not the case, though they do tend to sleep much more in winter and rarely venture out of their sets in

Hedgehogs harbour a variety of parasites.

Badger cubs at play

bad weather. Hedgehogs, on the other hand, do go through a period of true hibernation. Hibernation differs from sleep in several ways but the most obvious is the slowing of the metabolism. Heartbeat slows to about one-tenth of normal rate. Adrenal glands, accordingly, almost cease working. Blood magnesium amounts increase and blood sugar levels decrease. Body temperature drops. Before these processes begin large amounts of body fats (of two types) are stored. 'Brown fat' is laid down in the back and chest areas, whereas 'white fat' accumulates in layers under the skin and around the digestive organs. White fat is the first to be 'burned up' during hibernation, brown fat being used later. (Study of humans, who also have deposits of brown fat, has indicated that brown fat is more valuable in keeping the body warm.) It may in fact be that brown fat is used last of all, when body temperatures begin to recover in spring. Although hedgehogs hibernate, there are many cases of sightings in December. Many become active again very early in the year. There is no hard and fast rule, but it seems that length and timing of hibernation are governed by individual metabolism and amounts of stored fat.

Hedgehogs

Hedgehogs (*Erinaceus europaeus*) are members of the insectivorous Erinaceidae. Hibernation is, presumably, a result of natural selection to meet the shortage of insect food during northern winters. Much has been written about the diet of hedgehogs. Tame animals relish bread and milk and this food may have been first provided by householders in the misguided assumption that wild hedgehogs drink milk, as there have been many (unauthenticated) stories about hedgehogs suckling milk from recumbent cows. It is possible that hedgehogs may have been seen lapping up milk squirted from full udders onto the ground but highly unlikely that hedgehogs could suckle from a cow. As has already been mentioned, they are also credited with the ability to carry off apples on their spines. But, so far as I know, no one has ever seen a hedgehog eat an apple and it may be that the hedgehogs with crabs on their spines had fallen onto the apples. (Hedgehogs often throw themselves off a wall or bank, rolled up in a ball to break their fall, as they seem reluctant to climb down from a height and prefer to throw themselves down.) In reality their food usually consists of slugs, spiders, earthworms and carrion, if available.

Unfortunately, hedgehogs often become carrion themselves when they attempt to cross roads in the course of their nightly rambles for food. Many motorists have never even seen a live hedgehog, but everyone is familiar with those tyre-flattened corpses that have become such a common sight on Britain's roads. Hedgehogs are killed crossing roads because instead of scuttling away they merely curl up into a ball, as they would at the approach of any other danger. A few years ago a theory circulated that fewer hedgehogs were being flattened by cars because the process of natural selection was being speeded up. Proponents of the theory argued that hedgehogs which curl up when confronted by danger would die out, whereas those which run away would survive to create a race of non-curling hedgehogs. But the slaughter on the roads continues and the theory is as yet unproved. Another danger for hedgehogs is the substitution of cattle grids in place of gates where country roads pass from fenced to unfenced land, since hedgehogs fall through the bars and cannot climb out. One way to prevent such accidents would be to provide cattle grids with hedgehog ramps, so the trapped creatures can escape. In fact, a society has been formed for this purpose.

Although hedgehogs do not fall prey to a wide range of predators, they are occasionally killed by foxes and badgers, who may pounce before the hedgehog has had time to roll into a tight ball. Those hard spines which make such a good suit of armour are, however, a distinct hindrance to sanitation. Since hedgehogs are unable to clean themselves, they must suffer from constant irritation and itchiness due to parasites hidden in their forest of spines. They have justifiably earned the reputation of being one of nature's lousiest creatures. One parasite, *Archaeopsylla erinacei*, is specific to hedgehogs and cannot survive on other animals or humans. In addition, hedgehogs are plagued by mites and by a tick, *Ixodea hexagonus*, and many suffer from a type of ringworm (a fungal infection) which causes baldness and crumbling of skin.

Even though hedgehogs are plagued by lice, were once eaten by gypsies and are now frequently exterminated on roads and as a result of farming operations, nevertheless they continue to thrive and there are no signs that the hedgehog population is in any danger.

Moles

'Mole catcher please call'. This message appears with amazing regularity by the roadside at a farm near where I live. Moles (*Talpa europae*) are often regarded as an agricultural pest, but on the credit side they have healthy appetites and spend most of their working hours hunting for wireworms and earthworms. Judged on the basis of food, their influence is neutral. However, on arable land they may disturb the roots of crops by their burrowing, although their tunnels are beneficial in aerating and draining soil in meadows and pastures. It is true that mole heaps make a field difficult to cut at hay-making or silage time – but if spread about as a top dressing, they provide a source of extra minerals leeched down from the surface by rain action. On the whole moles are in fact no more than a slight nuisance.

Moles are rarely seen above ground.

Various methods of control have been used by mole catchers, who are themselves a species in decline because mole catching no longer pays as it used to in the days when velvety, best-quality pelts were sold at a premium to be made into moleskin coats for ladies and jackets and caps for countrymen. Because the mole catcher may not call, many farmers do their own mole catching by using scissor traps in moles' subterranean tunnels or by placing strychnine-soaked worms in their runs. Since moleskins are no longer saleable goods, moles are displayed on fences as a warning to their comrades to keep away.

There is, however, little point in such an exercise, since it is doubtful whether moles can see much more than the difference between light and dark. Other senses are more acute, though their sense of smell is underdeveloped. Hearing ability is good, but unremarkable. The most sensitive organ appears to be the snout, which is covered in nerve-containing papillae. These sensitive nerves are used to detect food animals by touch and may, possibly, also act as detectors of vibrations. A mole's snout is so sensitive that there is a great deal of truth in the old story that a mole could be killed by a blow on the snout.

Moles use their tunnels for transport, food storage, eating, sleeping and breeding. Each mole has its own tunnel system and the sexes usually aggressive towards each other, meet only for mating in February and March

Otherwise, meetings are on a casual basis when two tunnel systems overlap. Most tunnel systems have one chamber for food storage, where living but disabled worms are kept as a food reserve in case of shortage. One species of worm – *Lumbricus terrestris* – is favoured. Moles bite their worms near the head to immobilise them so that they remain in the storage chamber in fresh condition until eaten.

Moles spend most of their life underground but may be seen on the surface during the summer, particularly when the youngsters are driven out of the family home by their mother. At this time the young moles are at their most vulnerable to predators, including buzzards, owls, foxes and herons. It is not usually realised that moles are a major item in

A mole's snout is extremely sensitive.

the diet of herons, which catch moles not only on the surface but also from their runs. Presumably herons are able to feel vibrations through their feet as moles tunnel nearby. I have seen a cairn terrier hunt moles very successfully by this method, too. Weasels are ideally adapted by virtue of their thin, sinuous bodies to enter mole runs and frequently attack moles underground.

The fox

Little good can be said of the red fox (*Vulpes vulpes*). These cunning, adaptable carnivores prey upon a wide variety of wildlife from

Foxes are always alert to danger.

worms to hares and pheasants. In season wild fruits are added to their menu, which is also supplemented by domestic chickens and the occasional spring lamb. Therefore, to the farmer and conservationist alike, there is little to commend the fox. But our judgements should not be based upon mere usefulness or whether an animal kills enough pests in order to make up for the sin of taking game birds and domestic animals. Surely, despite their crimes, some foxes are worth preserving because they are a part of our ecosystem and also may be enjoyed for their beauty and intelligence. Yet perhaps it is arrogant to assume that we could exterminate the fox. For centuries they have survived all Man's efforts. Though fox hunters have no intention

of controlling foxes, farmers have worked hard for their extinction. But all to no avail.

Fortunately for Britain's fox population, rabies has not yet crossed the English Channel. This horrific viral disease is endemic throughout Europe, where the red fox is said to be the main vector. When humans are infected – a rare event in Europe – madness and hydrophobia, ending in death, are the inevitable result unless vaccines are used soon after infection. These vaccines are not totally reliable and, as with other diseases, the best method of control is eradication of sources and vectors. In Europe there have been massive extermination programmes, but since a few foxes always survive and the fox populations expand outwards to fill un-colonised areas, there is a possibility that extermination actually speeds the spread of disease. So a better method of rabies control may be to administer an oral vaccine hidden within carcases left out as bait in areas where there are fox colonies. Fortunately we are not yet faced with such a problem in Britain.

Foxes, long thought of as solitary animals, often live in groups with a social hierarchy. Usually there is only one dog to a colony of several vixens. Not all vixens have cubs and cubless vixens lower in the social scale sometimes act as aunts by providing extra meat once their dominant sisters' cubs have been weaned. Groups in an area are often loosely connected and some foxes spend their lives as gypsies, wandering from one colony to another. There seems little purpose in this except that the wanderers can, presumably, form a new community if an old one has been wiped out. Wandering may also be a response to inadequate food supplies.

Rodents

Rodents are the most abundant mammals of fields, farms and hedgerows. Their jaws are particularly well adapted for gnawing vegetation, seeds and nuts. At the front of the jaw are long incisor teeth, chisel-shaped for slicing off suitably sized pieces of food or for gnawing through hard seed coatings to reach the softer parts inside. Behind the incisor teeth there are no canine teeth – just a gap, with strong molars in the rear for grinding. A peculiarity of rodents is their need to keep using their incisor teeth, otherwise incisors may extend to such a length that they grow round in a circle or pierce the opposite jaw. Constant wear and tear is needed to keep teeth trimmed. Rodents often bite off more than they can chew. In other words, they store food by biting off suitably sized pieces which are carried off (in pouches in some rodents) to be stored away for winter use.

In earlier chapters we have seen how rat and mouse populations declined as better grain harvesting and storage techniques were introduced. Field voles (*Microtus agrestis*) have been relatively little affected by changing farming practices, but their populations do fluctuate to an enormous extent. Every four years or so, vole populations reach 'plague' proportions, with a consequent increase in the breeding success of owls and birds of prey. A year or two after a plague, populations suffer a severe reversal and vole predators also suffer a decline.

Field voles inhabit hedge banks and meadowland, where they construct communication routes and tunnels through long grass. Their nests are built above or below ground. Breeding takes place from spring to autumn. After mating and conception there is a 21-day gestation period before the blind, naked young voles are born. In two to three weeks the young are weaned and fully active.

Our other native vole found in farmland is the bank vole, a species which requires more cover than the field vole. *Clethrionomys glareolus* may be distinguished from the dull-brown field vole by its brighter upper coat, which tends to be of a shorter length than that of its cousin. Bank voles do not usually attain the same body weight as field voles (30–40 grams), but the feature which distinguishes them most readily is tail length. The tail of the bank vole is noticeably longer – being about half the length of its body, in contrast to the field vole's tail which is only one-third of its body length.

Harvest mice (*Micromys minutus*) are characteristically depicted by artists clinging to stalks of corn in a cornfield. This is not the only place where they are to be seen, for our smallest mammal may inhabit any area of long grass where it can weave a nest among the stalks and climb about foraging for seeds, using its prehensile tail to grasp nearby stalks for balance. In winter, after winds and heavy rain have flattened its summer territory, the harvest mouse may be found amongst bales of hay or in abandoned birds' nests in hedgerows.

Opposite Poised for flight, a fox straddles a wall.

Above Field vole

Breeding may continue for the greater part of the year from early spring to late autumn. Since the mice reach sexual maturity at about seven weeks of age, there are good opportunities for large population increases in years of plentiful food. Gestation lasts for about eighteen days, after which the usual blind, naked young rodents are born. The youngsters grow quickly, being ready to leave the nest in less than two weeks. After a few more days they are left to their own devices by their parents. Such a rapid breeding cycle is indicative of low life expectation. Harvest mice live for months, rather than years. Although they do little crop damage, harvest mice act as carriers of a virus disease which may be transmitted to man from contaminated grain.

Left Short-tailed or field vole

Below Harvest mouse

Study techniques

Various study techniques may be used, but small mammals are particularly evasive and the only sign one can expect is a rustling and slight movement of grass. One of the best methods for study is to use a Longworth mammal trap which, if used correctly, provides a safe and comfortable environment until the naturalist returns. If a supply of food and bedding material is supplied, the Longworth trap enables naturalists to study small mammal populations without harming them. A tripping mechanism, halfway down the chamber, closes the front entrance, trapping the animal within. Some small rodents enjoy their free bed and breakfast so much that they return to the trap regularly. Traps should not be left for a long period of time without attention and careful notes should be made of species, weight, sex and other relevant details, as described in the guidelines provided in other chapters.

Larger mammals are more difficult to trap but may be observed with the help of a lot of patience. There is nothing for it but to sit downwind of a badger set at dusk and await events. Foxes are often so inconspicuous as to be impossible to see until disturbed. Stoats and weasels carry on their activities more openly and you are bound to see them if you are willing to spend enough time in the countryside.

FURTHER READING

1 The shaping of the land

Body, R., *The Triumph and the Shame* (Temple Smith, 1982).
Bonnett, H., *Saga of the Steam Plough* (Allen & Unwin, 1965).
Bonser, K. J., *The Drovers* (Macmillan, 1970).
Cole, G. D. H., and Postgate, R., *The Common People* (Methuen, 1964).
Ernle, Lord, *English Farming Past and Present* (Longman, Green, 1912).
Evans, G. E., *The Pattern under the Plough* (Faber, 1966).
Freethy, R., *The Making of the British Countryside* (David & Charles, 1981).
Glob, P. V., *The Bog People* (Paladin, 1963).
Hammond, J. L. and H., *The Village Labourer* (Longmans, 1911).
Henderson, G., *The Farming Ladder* (Faber, 1952).
Mellanby, K., *Farming and Wildlife*, New Naturalist series (Collins, 1981).
Pye-Smith, C., and Rose, C., *Crisis and Conservation – Conflict in the British Countryside* (Pelican, 1984).
Raistrick, A., *Old Yorkshire Dales* (Pan, 1967).
Raistrick, A., *The Pennine Dales* (Eyre Methuen, 1978).
RSPB, *Farming and Wildlife* (RSPB, 1970).
Stamp, D., *Nature Conservation in Britain* (Collins, 1969).
Taylor, C., *Fields in the English Landscape* (Dent, 1975).
Trevelyan, G. M., *British History in the Nineteenth Century and After* (Longman, 1967).
Urquhart, J., *Animals on the Farm* (Macdonald, 1983).
Weller, J., *History of the Farmstead* (Faber, 1982).
Wightman, R., *The Countryside Today* (Pelham, 1970).

2 Birds

British Ornithologists' Union, *The Status of Birds in Britain and Ireland* (Blackwell, 1971).
Bruun, B., and Singer, A., *Birds of Britain and Europe* (Hamlyn, 1970).
Freethy, R., *How Birds Work* (Blandford, 1982).
Fuller, R. A., *Bird Habitats in Britain* (Poyser, 1982).
Heinzel, H., Fitter, R., and Parslow, J., *The Birds of Britain and Europe* (Collins, 1972).
Howells, G., 'The Status of the Red-legged Partridge in Britain', *Annual Report of the Game Reserve Association*, vol. 2 (1963), pp. 46–51.
Lorenz, K., *King Solomon's Ring* (Methuen, 1952).
Murton, R. K., *Man and Birds* (Collins, 1971).
Nicholson, E. M., *Birds and Men*, New Naturalist series (Collins, 1951).
Peterson, R., Mountfort, G., and Hollom, P. A. D., *A Field Guide to the Birds of Britain and Europe* (Collins, 1959).
Sharrock, J. T. R., *The Atlas of Breeding Birds in Britain and Ireland* (British Trust for Ornithology/ Poyser, 1976).
Sparks, J., and Soper, T., *Owls* (David & Charles, 1970).
Willett, W., *British Birds* (Black, 1948).

Witherby, H. F., Jourdain, F. C. R., Ticehurst, N. F., and Tucker, B. W., *The Handbook of British Birds* (Witherby, 1938–41).

3 Insects and invertebrates
Brian, M. V., *Ants*, New Naturalist series (Collins, 1977).
Burton, J., *The Oxford Book of Insects* (OUP, 1968).
Colyer, C. N., and Hammond, C. O., *Flies of the British Isles* (Warne, 1951).
Darlington, A., *Plant Galls* (Blandford, 1968).
Evans, H. E., and West Eberhard, M. J., *The Wasps* (David & Charles, 1970).
von Frisch, K., *Bees: Their Vision, Chemical Senses and Language* (Cape, 1950).
Imms, A. D., *Insect Natural History* (Collins, 1947).
Jones, A. W., *Introduction to Parasitology* (Addison Wesley, 1967).
Linssen, E. F., *Beetles of the British Isles* (Warne, 1951).
Oldroyd, H., *The Natural History of Flies* (Weidenfeld & Nicholson, 1964).
Spradberry, J. P., *Wasps* (Sidgwick & Jackson, 1973).
Stokoe, W. J., *The Caterpillars of British Moths* (Warne, 1948).
Tweedie, M. W. F., *Pleasure from Insects* (David & Charles, 1968).
Vessey-Fitzgerald, B., *The World of Ants, Bees and Wasps* (Pelham, 1969).

4 Plants
Brightman, F. H., and Nicholson, B. E., *The Oxford Book of Flowerless Plants* (OUP, 1966).
Bulow-Olsen, A., *Plant Communities* (Penguin, 1978).
Clapham, A. R., Tutin, T. G., and Warburg, E. F., *Flora of the British Isles* (CUP, 1962).
Dimbleby, G., *Plants and Archaeology* (Baker, 1967).
Fitter, A., Fitter, R., and Blamey, M., *The Wild Flowers of Britain and Europe* (Collins, 1974).
Howes, F. N., *A Dictionary of Useful and Everyday Plants and Their Common Names* (CUP, 1974).
Keble Martin, W., *The Concise British Flora* (Ebury/Michael Joseph, 1965).
Lang, D., *The Wild Flower Finder's Calendar* (Herridge, 1983).
Lousley, J. E., *Wild Flowers of Chalk and Limestone* (Collins, 1969).
McClintock, D., and Fitter, R. S. R., *The Pocket Guide to Wild Flowers* (Collins, 1956).
Prime, C. T., *Plant Life* (Collins, 1977).
Salisbury, Sir E., *Weeds and Aliens* (Collins, 1961).
de Sloover, J., and Goossens, M., *Wild Herbs, a Field Guide* (David & Charles, 1983).
Stokoe, N. J., *Grasses, Sedges and Rushes* (Warne, 1942).
Usher, G., *A Dictionary of Plants Used by Man* (Constable, 1974).
Vetvicka, V., *Wildflowers of Meadows and Marshes* (Hamlyn, 1981).

5 Trees and shrubs
Boulton, E. H. B., *British Trees* (Black, 1937).
Brough, J. C. S., *Timbers for Woodwork* (Evans, 1947).
Clapham, A. R., *The Oxford Book of Trees* (OUP, 1975).
Darlington, A., *Plant Galls in Colour* (Blandford, 1968).
Edlin, H. L., *Trees, Woods and Man*, New Naturalist series (Collins, 1956).
Edlin, H. L., *Collins Guide to Tree Planting and Cultivation* (Collins, 1970).
Hart, C., and Raymond, C., *British Trees in Colour* (Michael Joseph, 1973).
Mitchell, A., *A Field Guide to the Trees of Britain and Northern Europe* (Collins, 1974).
Rackham, O., *Trees and Woodland in the British Landscape* (Dent, 1976).

6 Mammals

Bishop, I., *Thorburn's Mammals* (Mermaid Books, 1983).

Boyle, C. L. (ed.), *RSPCA Book of British Mammals* (Collins, 1981).

van den Brink, F. H., *A Field Guide to the Mammals of Britain and Europe* (Collins, 1967).

Burton, J. A., *The Guinness Book of Mammals* (Guideway Publishing, 1982).

Burton, M., *The Hedgehog* (Deutsch, 1969).

Freethy, R., *Man and Beast* (Blandford, 1983).

Lawrence, M. J., and Brown, R. W., *Mammals of Britain: Their Tracks, Trails and Signs* (Blandford, 1967).

Lockley, R. M., *The Private Life of the Rabbit* (Deutsch, 1964).

Mellanby, K., *The Mole*, New Naturalist series (Collins, 1971).

Neal, E., *Badgers* (Blandford, 1977).

Sheail, J., *Rabbits and their History* (David & Charles, 1971).

Svendsen, P., *An Introduction to Animal Physiology* (MTP, 1974).

ACKNOWLEDGEMENTS

The production of this book would have been impossible without the help of the editor of the series, Ron Freethy, and his wife Marlene who typed the manuscript. Carole Pugh provided some excellent line drawings and I am also greatly indebted to the photographers mentioned below.

PICTURE CREDITS

Colour and Black & White Photos

Richard Abernethey: *page* 74 (top)
Will Bown: *pages* 43, 59, 68 (right)
Michael Chesworth: *pages* 13, 91 (top), 106, 112
John Clegg: *pages* 55 (bottom right), 89 (left), 90
Michael Edwards: *pages* 39, 55 (top), 91 (bottom), 93, 104 (top), 114, 118, 120
Robin Fletcher: *pages* 51 (bottom), 52
Ron Freethy: *pages* 16 (both), 77, 103, 115
E. C. M. Haes: *pages* 61, 65, 68 (left)
Robert Howe: *pages* 26 (both), 34, 36, 39, 42, 60 (bottom left and right), 104 (bottom), 107, 116, 119, 120 (top)
Brian Lee: frontispiece, *pages* 10 (both), 14 (both), 15, 18 (both), 19 (both), 22, 23, 24, 27, 30, 31, 35 (both), 46, 47, 54, 55 (both), 59 (bottom), 62, 63 (both), 66, 67 (both), 70, 71 (both), 78 (both), 79 (both), 80, 82 (both), 86, 94 (both), 95 (both), 98 (both), 99, 108, 111
Charles Linford: *pages* 29, 33, 41
Barry Ogden: *pages* 51 (top), 59 (top), 74 (top)
P. H. Ward: *page* 45
Bill Wilkinson: *pages* 10 (top), 84

Cover Photos

Top left: Michael Edwards
Top right: Michael Edwards
Bottom left: Barry Ogden
Bottom right: Brian Lee

Line Drawings

The line illustrations on pages 32, 37, 49, 75, 87, 102 and 109 are by Carole Pugh, and the diagram on page 45 was drawn by Vic Giolitto.

INDEX